Student Writing:
Give it a Generous Reading

Student Writing:
Give it a Generous Reading

By
Lucy K. Spence
University of South Carolina

INFORMATION AGE PUBLISHING, INC.
Charlotte, NC • www.infoagepub.com

Library of Congress Cataloging-in-Publication Data

The CIP data for this book can be found on the Library of Congress website (loc.gov).

Paperback: 978-1-62396-652-2
Hardcover: 978-1-62396-653-9
eBook: 978-1-62396-654-6

Copyright © 2014 Information Age Publishing Inc.

All rights reserved. No part of this publication may be reproduced, stored in a retrieval system, or transmitted, in any form or by any means, electronic, mechanical, photocopying, microfilming, recording or otherwise, without written permission from the publisher.

Printed in the United States of America

CONTENTS

	Introduction	vii
1.	Responding to Writing	1
2.	Generous Reading Method	11
3.	Insights into Writing	21
4.	Speakers of Other Languages	35
5.	Language Variation	45
6.	Writing Across the Curriculum	55
7.	Teachers Working Together	63
8.	Cuturally Relevant Instruction	71
9.	Language Transfer	79
10.	Literary Devices	87
	Appendix	95
	References	103
	Author Biography	107
	Index	109

INTRODUCTION

As a child, I drew and wrote on the back of used office paper my father brought home from his office. In elementary school, I wrote reports on Ireland, airplanes, and ceramic pottery. I also wrote a poem about the valley where I grew up, "I am encircled in arms of rock," a metaphor for mountains. These writing experiences deeply influenced my work as a teacher and researcher.

CONTEXT OF THE RESEARCH STUDIES

The process and product of writing have always interested me, but never more than when I studied under Joseph Tobin at Arizona State University. One day in class, he passed out a piece of student writing titled, "Last Day of Mexico," and we analyzed this story using all kinds of interesting techniques. I was fascinated by what I learned about the student who wrote the story and the interesting way she appropriated language to construct it.

Since reading "Last Day of Mexico," I have embarked on three research projects analyzing student writing. The first involved collecting writing from a 3rd-grade classroom in Arizona and analyzing each piece of writing using the tools I learned from Tobin (2000). Then I compared what I learned about each piece of writing to discern which tools worked best for

Student Writing: Give It a Generous Reading, pages vii–x.
Copyright © 2014 by Information Age Publishing
All rights of reproduction in any form reserved.

understanding student writing. From this analysis, I created the generous reading form.

When I moved to South Carolina, I began a second research project. This involved teaching the generous reading technique to five 5th-grade teachers and working with them to analyze their students' writing over the course of one year. In addition, I observed and interviewed one teacher to see how generous reading fit with her instruction of English learners.

A third project involved collecting the writing of students who speak various world languages such as Spanish, Karen, Chinese, Arabic, and Japanese. I am currently using generous reading to analyze these texts. Working with other educators to analyze writing in various world languages is both challenging and rewarding.

These three research projects resulted in many pieces of writing from a diversity of students. My original study included Latina/o students, European American students, Spanish speakers, English learners, and native English speakers. The second study included African Americans, European Americans, Latina/o students, Spanish speakers, southern English speakers, native English speakers, and English learners. The third study expanded my writing samples to world languages. I am finding that cultural and linguistic diversity in writing is a limitless treasure to explore. No actual student or teacher names were used in this book, except in the rare instance when participants wanted their names to be used.

A CLOSER LOOK AT RESEARCH

A number of composition scholars have explored writing through a postprocess paradigm (Harris, 1997; Heard, 2008; Kent, 1999). This moves beyond a product view of writing, which highlights mastering a body of knowledge (Breuch, 2002), and a process view, which highlights a recursive cycle including prewriting, drafting, revising, editing, and publishing (Calkins, 1983; Graves, 1983; Murray, 1968). In contrast, postprocess scholarship shifts away from the notion that there is one universal composition process. Rather, writing is seen as an interpretive practice, situated in a social context. It involves a public interchange, so the writer is never alone but is influenced by the sociocultural world.

In a postprocess view, the social context surrounding writing influences writers as they negotiate their place within communities outside of class and in class. The focus of postprocess pedagogy is upon a dialogic curriculum in which students and teacher talk and write for social purposes that are meaningful to the community. The teacher is not a dispenser of knowledge or a director of process. The teacher is a member of a community who engages in dialogue and writing alongside the students.

Researchers and teachers of children's writing have also moved beyond the product and process models of writing instruction. Anne Haas Dyson

(2003) describes social and cultural influences on children's texts, uncovering how children relate to the world through engaging in writing as they talk and write with their friends. Several scholars have explored children's writing as socially constructed texts, analyzing the writing as they would a respected piece of literature (Armstrong, 2006; Bomer, 2010). This focus on children's writing as meaningful work suggests a significant shift in how we regard children's writing.

ANALYZING WRITING

My research builds on postprocess scholarship and adds to current research on children's writing. In developing generous reading (Spence, 2008, 2010b), I used a variety of interpretive techniques borrowed from literary studies, critical theory, and cultural studies. These techniques included binary opposites (Lévi-Strauss, 1955), slips or double-voiced speech (Voloshinov, 1976), parody or citationality (Bakhtin, 1981), and metaphor (Lakoff & Johnson, 1980).

The initial research for developing generous reading was based on 15 students and 33 pieces of writing, including narrative, informational, and persuasive essays. These writings were collected throughout one school year from one classroom in which the teacher taught all subject areas. I analyzed these to find out which of the interpretive techniques were most useful.

The second project was based on writing from nine classes in which 61 students received parental consent to participate. In this study, the teachers and I analyzed their students' writing together. Some of these teachers taught all subject areas and some only two subjects.

In the third study, bilingual educators and I analyzed five students' writing in Chinese, Japanese, Spanish, Arabic, or English (by a speaker of Karen who does not write in her home language). In all three studies, I conducted observations and/or interviews to understand the context in which each piece was written.

I first read each piece holistically, then again using the interpretive techniques listed above or the generous reading form. After analyzing each piece, I went back to my field notes and interviews to cross-check the analysis and corroborate with the classroom context and other information. I shared each piece with other educators to gain additional perspectives.

The three research studies served to develop a novel approach to student writing that results in changes in how teachers view student writing (see Chapter 7, *Teachers Working Together*, this volume). My intention is to provide a view of student writing that takes into account students' relations with their communities and how writing is a part of the ongoing negotiation of ideas and identity that people experience in social interaction.

OVERVIEW OF THE CHAPTERS

Generous reading does not stand alone as a collection of analytical tools. It connects with culturally relevant pedagogy, linguistic research, and writing instruction. The chapters in this book deal with each of these topics, linking generous reading to issues that are important to writing teachers.

The first three chapters describe how to use generous reading. They give a rationale for taking the time to look closely at student writing and then walk the reader through the process, providing examples along the way. You will see how generous reading will inform your writing instruction by locating a student's learning zone.

Chapters 4 and 5 show how generous reading is useful for students who speak world languages or different varieties of English. These chapters provide information on linguistic diversity and language variation. The information has a practical side, with ideas for instruction in both chapters.

Chapters 6 and 7 explore teachers' use of generous reading. Chapter 6 describes what happened when teachers used generous reading for math, science, and history writing. This description is followed by ideas for instruction. Chapter 7 invites you into the after-school meetings of five teachers as they learned to use generous reading. This chapter reveals insights into writing and writing instruction informed by great (teacher) minds working together.

Once you have learned all about generous reading in the previous chapters, you are ready to connect it to the bigger picture. Chapters 8 and 9 link generous reading to research in culturally relevant pedagogy and linguistics. These topics add to our understanding of how students learn based on their cultural knowledge and their current language abilities. An enhanced understanding of culture and language will inform your generous reading.

Chapter 10 is the final chapter, a compilation of literary elements that will help you dig even deeper into student writing. Once you are hooked on finding these elements in your students' writing, you will want to learn more. The appendices that follow will give you everything you need to analyze writing—from the generous reading form to additional resources that can feed your knowledge of the limitless social, cultural, literary, and linguistic elements contained in writing.

This book would not exist were it not for the generosity of the students and teachers who participated in the development of generous reading. My sincere thanks go to each one of them.

CHAPTER 1

RESPONDING TO WRITING

Juan, a 3rd-grade student, wrote a story telling about a party he and his family attended. What do you notice about this piece?

> I had so much fun that I needed to caught my breath and it was already night time. but I still didn't leave yet because my mom and dad were still talking to someone. but two hour later we left and we got a candy bag.

You may have noticed that Juan had an awful lot of fun at the party, perhaps because of the phrase, "caught my breath." When we read to be entertained, emotionally moved, or to learn, we read generously, with the understanding that the author has something meaningful to say. We expect to engage in a meaningful transaction with the written word. On the other hand, we sometimes approach student writing differently than other things we choose to read. We may assume there will be something that demands correction. For instance, in this excerpt, Juan misspelled "catch." This might cause us to momentarily lose the flow of the narrative and focus on the misspelling instead the mood Juan is trying to convey. Too often, our first inclination is to focus on mistakes, and after years of hypercorrected writing, students often develop negative feelings toward writing and a reluctance to write.

Student Writing: Give It a Generous Reading, pages 1–10.
Copyright © 2014 by Information Age Publishing
All rights of reproduction in any form reserved.

There are however many teachers who focus on the writer's meaning and implement pedagogy that downplays correction and highlights positive feedback, cooperative revision, and a view of writing as a process. In this view, the text is not seen as a product but as one snapshot of the writer's growing ability. Juan's teacher, Karla, took this stance when she gave him a fairly high score for using correct conventions even though she expected him to improve in his future writing.

Karla saw writing as a developmental process wherein students over time come ever closer to standardized writing practices. She accepted Juan's approximations toward conventional writing. In subsequent teaching, she took his English language development into consideration by clearly explaining concepts, demonstrating, and continually monitoring his learning throughout the writing process.

The two approaches to Juan's writing described above are indicative of attitudes toward student writing in schools today. For some, the deficits in the writing are the focus. And for others, the message being communicated is most significant. As teachers, we want students to write, and we want them to learn to write well. Our response to their writing will either encourage or discourage writing. Our response should also show our students what they are doing well and what they can do better.

The purpose of this book is to describe a method of responding to student writing, which I call *generous reading*. It is based on three research studies. The writing samples in this book were taken from these studies, with the consent of the children and their parents.

In this chapter, I will explain why it was necessary to develop a new method for responding to linguistically diverse student writing. Then I will define generous reading, explaining the origins of the concepts involved. Last, I will discuss how the inherent diversity in the English language can enhance our response to student writing.

THE RUBRIC APPROACH

Regardless of teachers' stance toward writing instruction, they often feel pressured by national, state, district, and school mandates to evaluate writing in particular ways. For instance, Juan, who was a fairly advanced English speaker, was assessed with the same rubric as his classmate Rosa, who was a developing English learner. Karla consistently gave Rosa very low scores for her writing based on a rubric that was written for native English speakers. Like Juan, Rosa wrote about a special time with her family.

> Chrimes is a fun day becose you Get prsents. you have to put the Crismas tree and put the prents on the tree and put the litghts on the house you could see the litghs at the nigth. Then you do food and some copcake and some cookies or cake.

Rosa is clearly trying out hypotheses in her spelling. English spelling requires mastery of many different silent letter combinations in the words "Christmas" and "lights," whereas Spanish is spelled more regularly and phonetically. It is difficult to look past surface errors such as spelling when assessing writing, and often children who misspell end up with low scores.

Karla gave Rosa low scores for this paper with the exception of voice, which received a 4 on a scale of 1 through 6. The other scores were: Ideas and Content, 3; Organization, 3; Word Choice, 2; Sentence Fluency, 1; and Conventions, 2. Giving low rubric scores is a form of negative feedback, which students internalize as they develop an image of themselves as writers. Using numbers to describe writing sends a message about the writer. Think of the phrases, "On a scale of 1–10, he is a 3," "He is a C student," "She failed English." When we describe writing with numbers, we run the risk of labeling the writer. We also fail to take into account the fact that the writer is engaging in a process in which writing may be revisited and improved. Learning to write is a developmental process, especially for English learners. Rosa's writing will improve as she matures and as her command of the English language improves. Learning to write for the rubric cannot replace the process of learning a new language.

Of course, the rubric used in Karla's school district is not intended to label students. It is intended for both assessment and instruction. Teachers explicitly teach the traits of writing measured by the rubric. After teachers have scored student writing, the scores are discussed with students in terms of how the student can improve by attending to the rubric descriptors in future writing. Because Karla's rubric is made up of six pages of small print, it can be overwhelming to English learners.

The rubric approach to assessment is problematic for English learners for several reasons. The language may not be understood by English learners. The rubric descriptors do not take language learning into account. The rubric was designed for native English speakers. When a rubric is designed for fluent English speakers, how can we expect that language learners will be ready to write in a manner that includes all the descriptors?

I propose that teachers and students might benefit from an alternate way of approaching students and their writing. What would happen if instead of reading to determine a numerical score, we read to be entertained, to be moved, or to learn from students? What would happen if we read to find literary art, emotional insight, or valuable information in their writing? What would happen if we read to know our students in multiple ways—socially, culturally, and politically? What would happen if we read more generously, trusting that the writer has something meaningful to convey? Might it encourage a sense of risk, confidence, and challenge in our students?

When I read Juan's writing in this way, I imagined a hoard of kids running and laughing, playing active games outdoors at twilight with no thought of school, homework, or chores. I could hear Juan panting for breath when his mother caught him and told him it was time to go home. Then I imagined Juan's exuberant joy when he realized his parents had drifted back into a long conversation with their friends. I can see him hopping in place with anticipation as he waits in a crowd of children to receive his candy bag.

When I read Rosa's writing generously, I picture a dark night, sprinkled with stars, and Rosa's house strung with brightly colored lights. Inside, I can see the tree with presents stacked underneath, and I can almost smell the cookies and cakes baking in the oven. We do not often allow ourselves to interact with student writing, bringing our imagination into play with our students' words. Yet taking the time to interact with their writing will reveal the imagination, creativity, and language work of students.

DEFINING GENEROUS READING

All students deserve to have their writings read with care, imagination, and understanding—a generous reading. I have borrowed this phrase, "generous reading," for my approach to student writing. In other contexts, generous reading is a phrase used informally to describe readings of law, patient therapy, literature, as well as student writing. It expresses the act of uncritically reading a text but does not denote a specific methodology for doing so.

Literary scholars at times will take a generous rather than critical stance in reading a novel, or philosophers may take a generous stance in reading a philosophical work. From this tradition, some teachers of writing have adopted a practice of reading student texts closely, yet respectfully, as described by Donohue (2008): "Reading of student work *as writing*, that is, as legitimate text, with the assumption that it does make sense, carries its own internal logic, is justifiably studied as any other text, literary or expository" (p. 323).

A close reading of student writing reveals purposeful thinking. Armstrong (2006) uses descriptive and interpretive inquiry to demonstrate how children's writing follows the same purposes and procedures as literary masterpieces. He employs "sympathetic scrutiny" in a close reading of their texts informed by knowledge of the writer's context. Although the idea of generous reading has been around for a long time, it has never been described as a methodology for reading student writing.

In this book, I will explore ways of reading generously, drawing upon the writings of 20th century Russian philosopher Mikhail Bakhtin (1981, 1986), whose work is helpful in looking at writing with a renewed imagination. Two elements of generous reading I propose are defined by Bakhtin's notions of hybrid language and answering student writing. As teachers, our responsibility upon reading our students' work is to answer it. Not by rating it but by responding in a genuine and meaningful way. To do so, we must consider the many "hybrid" sources that students draw upon for writing.

HYBRID LANGUAGE

When we take time to look closely at student writing, we will find a hybrid text, containing seeds from many different sources, which are combined during the writing process to form a unique statement. As a student embarks upon writing, the immediate and historical context makes up the material, which is combined and developed into the written work.

Influences on student writing come from many contexts. Students bring something to their writing from their communities, cultural background, peers, and popular culture, drawing upon the rich mix of voices that surround them. Sports teams, song lyrics, playground games, and videogames make their way into writing. Phrases used by family members and slogans heard on television, the Internet, movies, and radio show up in writing. Local culture adds richness to student writing as in the following excerpt from a student living on a coastal sea island in the Deep South.

> Wow as I walk onto the marsh board walk I see different type of things. Like fiddler crabs they are little tiny Baby crabs and raccoon prints. They come for fresh air. Also I see plants and snails crawling on them.

In this short excerpt describing the nearby salt marsh, the student draws upon the voices of popular culture, his teacher, his science book, and his own experience seeing the little, tiny, baby crabs.

Student writing is usually influenced by teachers and classmates. As students and teachers discuss topics in class, these discussions make their way into stories, reports, and essays. We are all familiar with seeing quotes or paraphrases from books integrated into writing. How many times have we despaired over material that is copied directly from a book? Learning to skillfully cite sources is an essential part of the writing curriculum, although students don't always use sources in ways we can predict. Direct or indirect citation of books and other texts are often found in student writing.

The current economic and political climate also impacts elements of writing such as topic choice and tone. Student writing is affected by national, state, and district mandates such as writing prompts used in state assessments to which students must conform. Current national and world events can make their way into writing. After the September 11, 2001, terrorist attacks, I collected student writing with references to the World Trade Center Towers. In writing about his experience sitting in the top row at a movie theater, a student wrote, "I feel like I'm sitting on a high mountain or giant twin-tower."

TABLE 1.1. Bakhtin's Concepts Used In Generous Reading

Concept	Definition
Voice	A reflection of the values behind the speaker or writer.
Dialogue	The inherent nature of language: response and expectation of a response.
Hybrid Language	The traces of other voices contained in language.
Answerability	The responsibility to engage in dialogue with others.

History also influences student writing. Juan and Rosa both wrote narratives, a "mode of discourse" that can be traced back to ancient Rome. Personal narratives have been popular assignments since the 1960s, when teachers began emphasizing student voice. When our students write, they engage in a dialogue with others in a stream of words that stretches from the historical past to the present act of writing and into an imagined future. Quotes, songs, slogans, and games are all part of the dialogue between past and present, home and school, the student and their world. Students write under the influence of many voices, both past and present, and with the expectation of a response, which Bakhtin refers to as answerability (see Table 1.1 for examples of Bakhtin's concepts used in generous reading).

ANSWERING WRITING

As writing teachers, we are an essential part of the dialogue between the student and their world because of our role as the primary audience for writing. Students have other audiences as well, such as their classmates, family, and community members, and all of these must answer the author in some way. This may take the form of directly talking with the author about the writing or may consist of taking in the message of the writing and incorporating the message at a later time.

Every speaker expects a response. Writers also need an active, responsive understanding as a result of their writing. Everything said or written is constructed in anticipation of a response. Thus, we have an important responsibility to answer student writing. In giving an answer, we participate in a dialogue with the student. This dialogue may have been initiated by the teacher by giving an assignment, or it may be initiated by the student in choosing to write for his or her own purposes. Either way, the student's part in this dialogue begins with joining a stream of voices in which others have spoken before. The student will draw upon voices of others for phrases or ideas to include in their written work. Upon reading the student's writing, we likewise join in the stream of dialogue and must add our own voice to that of the student and other voices within the writing.

Answering is dialogic, in contrast to assigning a grade or score. A grade or score is the final word, given by an authority seemingly uninterested in continuing a dialogue. A grade or score does not engage in the ideas expressed through writing. The grade or score shuts down communication by signaling an end to the discourse. It says, "The assignment is complete and this is my evaluation."

On the other hand, we may choose to answer student writing in ways that encourage continued communication. Once children have passed into the intermediate grades and continuing through university, they receive written feedback on a fairly continual basis. A common experience is for the teacher to write comments in the margins of a paper. By writing comments directly on a student's paper, the teacher enters a sort of dialogue by responding to the ideas found in the writing. However, it is left to the student to in some way answer the comments. From the student's side, an answer may be internalizing some of the comments, to be used in future writing. The student might also make immediate revisions to the paper. Of course, the student may not even read the comments, ending the intended dialogue.

Another method of giving feedback is to talk directly to the student. Teachers working within a writing workshop often confer face-to-face with students. This form of response is more dialogic than written comments because it allows for a true dialogue to emerge as the teacher and student talk about the piece of writing. Talking face to face, a teacher can point out elements that are especially effective. The teacher can ask questions about things that are not clear and encourage students to describe their thinking. A true dialogue allows both the teacher and student to think about the writing in new ways. In a dialogic writing conference, the teacher does not come to the conference with all the answers but is willing to listen and change initial perceptions of the writing based on what the writer has to say.

Some teachers make arrangements for peer response, giving students opportunities for engaging in dialogue with the writer and allowing for many voices to contribute to revisions. In order for peer response groups to be most effective, students must be guided toward offering constructive feedback to the writer, and the writer must be guided toward asking their peers for specific input.

Our choice of how to respond to student work is an important decision. Nondialogic response modes include numerical scores from a rubric, checklists of requirements, and letter grades. Dialogic response modes include individual conferences and peer group response. Peers may respond one-to-one with an individual, or larger groups can engage in dialogue about writing. In this example, an English-language teacher was working with Delia when they came upon a question that could be answered by others in the classroom. The teacher directed her question to everyone.

Teacher:	What did we talk about, beginnings? We can . . . [standing up and looking at the whole class] Can anybody help? What are we talking about beginnings? How can we write beginnings?
Cesar:	This is what—when we write. Use one of those words [points to chart on wall] to start a beginning.
David:	Like, ask a question.
Teacher:	Make it mysterious.
Cesar:	Make it exciting.
David:	Her wish. Have you ever made a wish before?
Delia:	Oh, that is good. Yeah! I think it's a good idea.

Peer dialogue is valuable to students because it gives them access to ideas they would not have thought of on their own, yet the suggestions do not come with the authority vested in a teacher. The student writer may feel free to take or leave suggestions given by a peer as in the conversation above. Yet conversations that generate and extend the writer's thinking provide a dialogic response to the writing and develop a sense of writing community.

LEARNING ENGLISH IS A PROCESS

We are all English learners in the sense that we continue to acquire new vocabulary, new understanding, and more control of the English language every time we listen, speak, read and write. Children who are acquiring English are also on the journey to ever-greater control of the English language. English is a complex language, developed through historical events over time. Invasions and conquests resulted in a mixture of German, French, Greek, and Latin influences on the language. Trade and migration have continually added to the depth and richness of English through African languages, Spanish, and other influences over the years. The English language is complex and ever-changing. It is spoken with subtle and not-so-subtle differences by people in many parts of the world. Regional differences are to be found in every English-speaking country.

To illustrate a local variety of English spoken and written in the southeastern sea islands, I quote a 5th-grade student writing an essay for the school's drug awareness campaign.

> Red Ribbon week educates kids on why not to try drugs not even once, because if you take drugs just even once you going to be hooked. And that's going to lead to stealing, then lying, then eventually just getting arrested. And I don't think living in a cell for years and years is worth some drug that only lasts 3 minutes or half an hour at the max.

This writing sample reflects African American English—"You going to be hooked"—as well as current popular American ways of speaking—"half an hour at the max." It reflects the changing nature of English spoken by a student who is learning to speak and write English at home, in the neighborhood, at school, and from popular media. If you are a writing teacher, you have a complicated and fascinating mission in navigating the diverse varieties of English in existence today.

As teachers of English, we must consider the journey our students are on. And we must consider their language context. Where are they in the process of learning English? What do they already know, and what could help them to move forward? Our task is to help students communicate clearly, and this can only be accomplished by first understanding the student's language background and what they are already doing with language. We must also be genuinely interested in the message the student is trying to convey. The more you understand about your students, the better equipped you will be to help them become more eloquent in expressing their thoughts.

The purpose of this book is to describe an alternative way of reading the writing of culturally and linguistically diverse students. Why should we read student writing this way? In my experience, generous reading transforms teachers' perceptions of their students as people, and as writers. The teachers I have worked with immediately begin to value student writing in new ways. The generous reading method includes literary analysis and sociocultural theory. These tools will aid you in expecting and looking for meaning in the student text. Students bring something valuable to their writing from their culture and their lives. They have something important to say about their experience and the world, in a critical and political sense. Generous reading involves considering the social and cultural context in a thoughtful and meaningful response; it answers the writing dialogically.

The following chapter describes the generous reading method and how to use it in the classroom. In later chapters, generous reading conducted by a variety of teachers will describe children from several language backgrounds: Latino students, African American students, and students new to the United States from a variety of countries as well as students who grew up speaking standardized English. Generous reading will illuminate these students as people who are developing the ability to enter into dialogue with the world around them and reveal something about each person's view of the world.

Each generous reading contained in this book was influenced by either my perception or the classroom teachers' perceptions. Other readers may find their own meanings in the children's texts because all readings are influenced by the knowledge and background the reader brings with them. Writing and responding are like a conversation, and no two conversations are alike. So my generous reading and your generous reading are never the final word but only one piece of the conversation. I invite readers to join with me in exploring student writing through generous reading. I have provided a blog space for you to post your own interpretations of these pieces of writing as well as generous readings of your own students' writing (generousreading.org).

CHAPTER 2

GENEROUS READING METHOD

At a state English teachers' conference, I had the opportunity to share generous reading with several teachers in an intimate setting. I asked them to bring some of their student writing with them. After I described the generous reading method, they began to read their student work. Soon, one of the teachers looked up at me with astonishment and said, "I brought this piece with me because I was really worried about this child, but now I can see all the amazing things he has experienced. I can see who he is through his writing." Since then, I have heard similar comments from teachers of all types, including middle school teachers, special education teachers, teachers of English learners, and teachers of very young children.

HOLISTIC READING

When I sit down with teachers to read student writing, we first read the whole piece from beginning to end, holistically. We don't evaluate it. We just read and see where the writing itself takes us. We read with an open mind because the writing may take us somewhere we didn't expect. I tell teachers to ignore the writing assignment, ignore the genre, and be open to surprises. How many times have students received a lower score because

Student Writing: Give It a Generous Reading, pages 11–19.
Copyright © 2014 by Information Age Publishing
All rights of reproduction in any form reserved.

their interpretation of the assignment was not what the teacher or test-maker intended?

Suppose we ask students to write a story about a family tradition. We might expect a story about Thanksgiving dinner, or birthday parties, yet one child writes a story about her sometimes scary, sometimes joyful experiences going to the theater where her mother cleans every week. Is the child's story any less absorbing or enlightening? Does a different interpretation of family tradition make the story better or worse? Sometimes we take our own biases about the nature of an assignment into our judgment of student writing, yet if our goals are for students to enjoy writing, to become better writers, and to write for a variety of purposes, we shouldn't be bound by assignment topics.

With your first reading, let go of preconceived notions of the assignment, the genre, and any other notions of what you want the writing to be and let the writing take you where it will. Some writing absorbs our attention. Some writing enlightens us about the student's life outside of school.

Generous Reading

Student	Date	Grade	Teacher
Genre	Process Stage	Title	

Voices of Others	Figurative or Descriptive Language
What are the voices in this piece?	What figurative or descriptive language is in this piece?

What does this tell you about the person?

What does this tell you about the writer?

What does this reveal about the piece?

What is the student doing especially well that I want to reinforce?

What can I teach that will help the student grow as a person or as a writer?

What can I teach that will help improve this piece or future writing?

Student notes: English learner (level), AAE Dialect, Gender.

FIGURE 2.1 Generous Reading Form

Other writing teaches us something new about a topic we know little about. Some writing is like poetry in its simplicity, while other writing is so dense with action, the writer may even forget periods and commas. Notice the action—do not dwell on the punctuation. Let the writing take you into the child's imagination or personal experiences. Let the child teach you something in a new way, even if you already know something about the topic. Look at the world through your student's eyes.

After you have read the piece all the way through, without biases or preconceived notions, you are ready to read it again using the generous reading form (Figure 2.1). You will begin by noting information about the student, which will be important for record keeping: date, grade, student name, and teacher. The next line on the form is to record the genre, the process stage, and the title. Generous reading can be used with a variety of genres such as personal narrative, memoir, character sketch, persuasive essay, biography, historical essay, and all types of fiction. Some teachers have even used it with math and science writing. It can be used at any time during the writing process, such as with a rough draft, a revision, or a finished piece of writing.

At the bottom of the form there is a space to record additional information about the student that is important to keep in mind for assessment. In this space you will write any language information you have, such as the English acquisition level. Also record information on the language test and form used since many language proficiency tests provide levels that mean different things on different tests. Also record other home language information related to regional dialect, or African American English. This information will help you appreciate the variety students bring to their writing. Finally, record the gender of the student. This information will allow other people to discuss the writing using the pronouns "she" or "he."

VOICES OF OTHERS

Now for the generous reading itself! Your first task is to think about all the possible voices you may hear in the writing as you reread the piece a second time. I list some types of voices you may find, but not all writing contains these. Try to notice the voices of other authors from the books the student has read. Sometimes books are cited and other times they are not, depending upon the age and writing savvy of the student. Also notice the voice of the teacher or classmates who have interacted with the student during the writing process or at other times during the school year.

Repeated ideas or phrases from the classroom may be found in student writing. Other voices found in writing may come from the media. Commercials, public service announcements, television shows, movies, videogames, and song lyrics are highly influential sources. Other aspects of popular culture might be brought into writing as well. Sports references, toys, games,

The narrative as Marisol wrote it	The narrative with correct conventions
The Quiecenera Girl	The Quinceañera Girl
My family traditons is a Quiece-nera. My family have 6 girls. every girl wears a white drees. I don't know why. I don't know want the church is call but it is nice and big The church outside is big to and inside it has glass of god and others to Them from there then lemo drops use at the party. The lemo is long and black inside it cool it like a hall wall. want we eat is call moixe food. we eat beams with rice and meat and sometime bread. We drink punch or sota. The give us forks, spoon, or a kniw. The chair are blue a white. so are the table and flowers. blue and white are the balloons to. The quice girl dances to a song with some one sometime she dances to my day little girl are a other song them every one danc. We danc to rap or spinank. Them we cute the cake the cake looks good it has rose and sometime is has lays it has frosting on it we eat at the same time the ice cream has all mix. Then we save the presents for last we get a lot of cards That said I hope you have a great day Then the people that could make it goes the next day and we eat mothewn with cofey.	My family tradition is a Quinceañera. My family has six girls. Every girl wears a white dress. I don't know why. I don't know what the church is called but it is nice and big. The church outside is big too, and inside it has glass of God and others too. Then from there the limo drops us at the party. The limo is long and black. Inside it is cool like a hall wall. What we eat is called Mexican food. We eat beans with rice and meat and sometimes bread. We drink punch or soda. They give us forks, spoon, or a knife. The chairs are blue and white. So are the table and flowers. Blue and white are the balloons too. The Quince Girl dances to a song with someone. Sometimes she dances to "My Daddy's Little Girl" or another song. Then everyone dances. We dance to rap or Spanish. Then we cut the cake. The cake looks good. It has roses and sometimes it has layers. It has frosting on it. We eat at the same time the ice cream, it has all mixed. Then we save the presents for last. We get a lot of cards that said, "I hope you have a great day." Then the people that could make it go the next day and we eat more then with coffee.

FIGURE 2.2. "The Quinceañera Girl"

and commercial businesses such as food franchises may be seen in writing. The voices of parents and other authority figures may be heard. Finally, ethnic culture may appear in the form of words or phrases from the home language, references to other countries or regions, special traditions, dress, food, music, and many other forms of culture.

When Marisol, a Mexican American 3rd-grade girl wrote about her sister's *quinceañera* (15th birthday celebration), which took place in a church, I pondered what she meant by the phrase, "Inside it had glass of God and others, too" (see Figure 2.2). Finally, I mentioned it to another teacher who said, "Could it be stained-glass windows?" Suddenly it was very obvious: Marisol did not know the English vocabulary, but she used the vocabulary she did have to describe the church in her own way. Students may also use words or phrases from their home language for the same reason. If they do not know a word in English, they may write the word in another language. Students sometimes use their home language because it is the best way to represent something. *Quinceañera* is the perfect word for Marisol to use for her sister's 15th birthday celebration and "The Quinceañera Girl" was the perfect title for the story.

LITERARY ELEMENTS AND DESCRIPTION

As we continue our generous reading, our next task is to search for literary elements and description in the writing. Literary elements are present in everyday speech, not just fancy words and phrases learned in English class. We commonly use metaphors, such as paper thin, pounding headache, and butterflies in my stomach. Children pick up these phrases by hearing them spoken in school and at home, on television, and in the community. Children also use literary elements such as alliteration, rhyme, and onomatopoeia simply because these things are a natural part of spoken language. As children compose, they can hear the beauty of a phrase such as, "lights in the night." They like the sound of writing that says bow-wow, bang, flip-flop, and cock-a-doodle-do! They will use words like this without knowing the formal names, but simply because it sounds right, even when English is not their first language.

Sometimes student writing will have descriptions, but not formal literary elements. It pays to attend to simple description as well. Words or phrases that surprise you or bring an idea into sharp focus should be recorded on the form. Some descriptive phrases I've noticed in children's writing are "little turtle," "people outdoors," "if I jump high." Paying attention to these simple descriptions led me to understand the students' writing in a deeper way. For example, "people outdoors" was one student's way of referring to the homeless. Record phrases such as these on your generous reading form.

16 • STUDENT WRITING: GIVE IT A GENEROUS READING

THE PERSON

Now that we have collected all the voices, literary elements, and descriptive language from our student writing, we can think about what it all means. What does this language tell us about the student as a person? How does she or he relate to others? What is important to him or her? What does the student understand about the world, the community, or human nature?

Generous Reading

Student		Date	Grade	Teacher
Marisol		W 2004	3	Ms. Karla
Genre	Process Stage		Title	
Personal Narrative	Final		The Quinceañera Girl	

Voices of Others	Figurative or Descriptive Language
What are the voices in this piece?	*What figurative or descriptive language is in this piece?*
I don't know why.	the limo drops us at the party
I don't know what the church is called.	glass of god
Daddy's little girl	it is like a whole wall
I hope you have a great day	save the presents for last
Save the presents for last	people that could make it

What does this tell you about the person?

Starting to view her tradition through the eyes of others. The church and party are outside of everyday reality. Intimately connected with the tradition although she is not herself the quinceañera girl. Sees herself as one day being the girl.
She is knowledgeable and responsible. She enjoys participating in the tradition. People are important.

What does this tell you about the writer?

Takes audience questions into consideration. Uses names, titles as details when she can Uses a quotation as a revealing detail. Uses imagery. Created a new metaphor
Uses language of the quinceañera expert and pop culture

What does this reveal about the piece?

Introduces an important detail in first paragraph. The story is organized in time order of the main aspects of the tradition. Second paragraph describes setting. There is imagery, theme, mood, metaphor and symbol. Details develop theme and mood are evident.

What is the student doing especially well that I want to reinforce?
Organization through time, descriptive detail, voice of an expert

What can I teach that will help the student grow as a person or as a writer?
Re-reading, ask if it sounds like someone would talk

What can I teach that will help improve this piece or future writing?
Teach re-reading as a strategy, Point out sentence where she used present tense, contrast with past tense in a t-chart

Student notes: English learner (level), AAE Dialect, Gender.
Emerging English learner TESOL levels, home language is Spanish, female

FIGURE 2.3. Generous Reading Form "The Quinceañera Girl"

In order to understand student writing, we must first delve into whom the student is from his or her own perspective. Halasek (1999) says, "Students cultivate their voices, not as writers, but as people engaged in the act of writing about their lives and their beliefs" (p. 46). Through the act of writing, students link themselves to larger contexts in the world around them and develop as social beings. The way in which students describe their world reveals their views and their understanding of their place in the world.

Reread the voices, literary elements, and description you found in the student writing and answer the question, "What does this tell you about the student as a person?" A generous reading of Marisol's essay, "The Quinceañera Girl" (see Figure 2.3), shows me that family is important to Marisol, she knows a lot about Mexican culture, and she has a great sense of responsibility. Through generous reading, I understand more about Marisol, and as a teacher I can help her build upon these personal strengths.

THE WRITER

Next we ask, "What does this tell us about the writer?" We know that students engage in a process as they write. According to Murray (1968), Graves (1983), and Calkins (1986), the process includes prewriting, drafting, revising, editing, and publication. These generalizations help us think about the process of writing. With generous reading, we want to see the details of how the student goes about writing. How is she generating ideas? Is she drawing on experience or outside resources? Is she using knowledge of her home language to help her construct English sentences? Is she generalizing what she knows about grammar as she experiments with language? This is a good time to think carefully about what the student is already doing and what she is on the verge of learning. By thinking about her process, you will be able to see what she can learn that will help her move forward in her writing.

Generous reading helped me see that Marisol positioned herself as an expert on the *quinceañera* by explaining the tradition in detail to her audience. She drew upon her knowledge of Mexican culture and pop culture in her description. She drew upon others through quotation. And most interestingly, generous reading helped me to see that Marisol used what she knew about the English language to create a new metaphor: "Glass of God."

THE WRITING ITSELF

Finally, we ask, "What does this tell us about the writing itself?" At this point, I like to go back to the student writing. I can now see the piece of writing with new eyes as I ask, "What is important for me as a teacher to know about this piece of writing?" Thinking about the voices and figurative language forced me to look closely at the writing. Going back to it, I can now see the strengths in organization, grammar, word use, mood, theme, paragraphs, and the myriad other things that make up a piece of writing. I only look for what is there, not what is missing, because as a teacher, I have to know what the student can do on her own before I can help her.

The first thing I noticed upon reading Marisol's essay this time was the organization. In describing her sister's *quinceañera*, Marisol presented the events in order, according to the time at which the events occurred. She described the church ceremony, then the reception, and finally the breakfast party the following day. Each paragraph has its own topic.

In addition, Marisol used sophisticated imagery, included symbolism, and developed a theme and mood. These are marvelous accomplishments for a 3rd-grade English learner. Marisol did not set out to use literary elements. She did not even start with writing an outline (although she did make a concept map). Rather, Marisol drew upon her experiences and what she knew about language to inform her audience about a beloved Mexican tradition. Use your generous reading notes and a second reading of the student writing to write what you notice about the writing itself.

We now know much more about our student as a person, a writer, and the writing itself. We are ready to take this information and decide what and how to teach our student. The three questions at the bottom of the form will help us think about what to do with this information. We first ask, "What is the student doing especially well that I want to reinforce? What can I teach that will help the student grow as a person or as a writer? What can I teach that will help improve this piece or future writing?"

The answers to these questions will depend upon your teaching goals, grade level expectations, the individual writing development of the student, and the student's language development. The following conversation illustrates how Marisol's teacher, working with a group of children, reinforced what Marisol was doing well in her piece.

Karla: This is so good, over here, look—this is so good, look at this. [Karla writes on the overhead, "Then we save the presents for last."] That is an important detail, saving the presents for last. Marisol, you are a quinceañera expert. You used what you know to write details about the quinceañera.

Student: Save the best for last.

Karla: [laughing] Save the best for last—I like that. It sounds like something your mother would say. Marisol, that is something you can ask yourself when you reread your writing. Ask, "Does that sound like what someone would say? Reread your story and find places where you write just like someone would say it."

The students in this writing group began rereading their stories and saying phrases aloud to see if they sounded like someone actually talking.

Karla used what she learned through generous reading to help Marisol see that she had many details to share about *quinceañera* because she was an expert on the subject. Karla often singled out children in their small groups or in the whole class to highlight a child's strengths. Karla also built upon Marisol's correctly worded sentence to teach a strategy for rereading written work. Through rereading, children can learn to monitor their own language use. This was especially important for Marisol because although she had internalized many English phrases, at times she still struggled with sentence structure. This strategy helped to develop an ear for English sentence construction. Rereading is both a writing strategy and a language-development strategy.

Now you have completed the generous reading form, from jotting notes about voices in the writing, literary elements, and descriptive language. You have thought about what the writing tells you about the student as a person and as a writer. You have noticed strengths in the writing. Hopefully, this process helped you to see student writing in a very different way than the usual corrective feedback view. Filling out the form provides a way to think more deeply about student writing. It helps in seeing the writing and the person with new eyes.

You may wonder about the length of time it will take to use this form with every student in your classroom. I recommend using the form with a small group of students during each grading period, starting at the very beginning of the school year. I would begin with the students who I am concerned with most. This will allow you to plan instruction using the form for the students who most need a positive boost to their confidence as writers.

There is a lot of information on this form; too much to use it all. In fact, it's better if we focus only on one or two things to use as teaching points. Karla did that by focusing on how Marisol described details with voice and perfect grammar. Karla took that focus to the next level by suggesting that Marisol and the other children reread their stories to find other places where they wrote the way a person actually talks. Although Karla chose to focus on these teaching points, her generous reading opened her eyes to many other aspects of Marisol as a person and as a writer.

CHAPTER 3

INSIGHTS INTO WRITING

Rosa walked into the classroom with her worn red notebook tucked among several library books. She took her place on the floor in the writing circle. Her teacher, Karla, asked, "Rosa, what will you write about lions?" Rosa looked thoughtfully at her teacher but was silent. A classmate, Lita, suggested, "Rosa, you can ask why they have fur all around their head." Soon Rosa had written almost a page in her red notebook, then began to confer with two girls seated nearby.

In this workshop environment, the girls moved easily from talking to writing. Later, Rosa again looked up from her writing to listen as her teacher demonstrated how to write research questions on a large sheet of chart paper. During the demonstration, Rosa looked down occasionally and added a word or two to her paper. When the other children went back to their tables, Rosa lingered over her paper. Then she wandered over to a table crowded with children, where she stopped to listen before circling back to her own table.

This is the way Rosa typically worked in her 3rd-grade writing workshop classroom. She expressed herself mostly through her writing or to her close friends. She did not speak up much in whole-class discussions, but listened and watched carefully. In this chapter, I will focus on Rosa in order to illustrate how to use a completed generous reading form to note aspects of

---

Student Writing: Give It a Generous Reading, pages 21–34.
Copyright © 2014 by Information Age Publishing
All rights of reproduction in any form reserved.

language students are controlling, how they are using knowledge from their first language, and what literary forms they have appropriated. I will describe how you can use this knowledge to locate a student's learning zone. Vygotsky (1986) described the zone of proximal development. This is the area of instruction the student is ready to move into and for which you plan instruction that will have the most effect on students' future writing. Additionally, I will illustrate why assessment must be sensitive to cultural and linguistic diversity.

ROSA, AN ENGLISH LEARNER

Rosa was born in the United States and grew up speaking Spanish at home. She understood English in simple, everyday situations, used simple grammatical structures correctly, and was beginning to use general academic vocabulary. She still produced basic errors in her written communication while experimenting with English grammar and spelling. This experimentation is evident in a personal narrative she wrote at the beginning of the school year, about a treasured family tradition. Her original writing is shown in Figure 3.1.

My Family Tradition

Christmas is a fun day because you get presents. You have to put the Christmas tree and put the presents on the tree and put the lights on the house. You could see the lights at the night. Then you do food and some cupcake and some cookies or cake. Then you could invite other people to come to your house and see a movie in the night and eat popcorn. And play a game or balloon splash. And you could have a fun day on Christmas because It is my best day ever. When it's time to open your presents you do a mess on your floor. Then we all sleep and the other people sleep on our house. Then we wake up and some people come and give us some presents. And when I open it was a Bratz. It is my best toy I like. The Bratz are my favorite toy to play. I play with them all the time. When I go to school I don't have time to play. I only play when there's no school. My parents give me some dolls. And we all go get a shower with my shampoo. And they give me a dress and some blusitas and a little baby toy. And to my sister they give her a baby toy and with a cuna. And to my small sister a baby and a shirt. It is pretty.

While assessing this piece, Rosa's teacher summed up Rosa's communication style: "She is very, very quiet. She hardly ever says a word, and this is probably the only way she communicates to me, and to other people, is in her writing." Her teacher was also sensitive to Rosa's English development, "She's a Spanish speaker, and these are the sounds that she hears. She follows the syllabication. Yes, she really is working hard to spell with the sounds that she hears." Karla's observation of Rosa's social interaction and learning style illustrates how essential observation is for authentic assessment. Generous reading complements such observations. Looking for voices and literary/descriptive language is another way of getting to know student writers.

My family Tradition original writing	My family tradition with correct conventions
(handwritten text)	My Family Tradition
	Christmas is a fun day because you get presents. You have to put the Christmas tree and put the presents on the tree and put the lights on the house. You could see the lights at the night. Then you do food and some cupcake and some cookies or cake. Then you could invite other people to come to your house and see a movie in the night and eat popcorn. And play a game or balloon splash. And you could have a fun day on Christmas because It is my best day ever. When it's time to open your presents you do a mess on your floor. Then we all sleep and the other people sleep on our house. Then we wake up and some people come and give us some presents. And when I open it was a Bratz. It is my best toy I like. The Bratz are my favorite toy to play. I play with them all the time. When I go to school I don't have time to play. I only play when there's no school. My parents give me some dolls. And we all go get a shower with my shampoo. And they give me a dress and some blusites. and a little baby toy. And to my sister they give her a baby toy and with a cuna. And to my small sister a baby and a shirt. It is pretty.

FIGURE 3.1. Original Writing "My Family Tradition"

NOTICING VOICES IN WRITING

When I approach Rosa's narrative looking for voices of others, I notice the voice of an expert at "doing Christmas." Rosa's purpose is to tell her audience step-by-step how to put up the tree, put lights on the house, prepare the food, invite guests, play games, and open presents. Her point of view is second-person narrative, "you have to put the Christmas tree." Rosa switches to first person when she says, "it is my best day ever." She uses plural pronouns to include others: "then we all sleep and the other people sleep on our house." From her experimentation with various voices, I see Rosa as an expert on Christmas who enjoys the holiday very much. I see the importance of family in her use of the collective "we." I also learn something about Rosa as a writer from her experimentation with pronouns. She uses second person to impart information, singular pronouns to portray her emotion, and plural form to advance the theme of family life.

I see other voices in her writing as well. Mexican culture and popular culture are evident in her use of *blusitas*, little blouses; *cuna*, cradle; *Bratz* a name-brand fashion doll; and *balloon splash*, a children's party game. These cultural references, along with her accompanying illustration (Figure 3.2) help me to see how Rosa blends many cultural aspects of her life as she portrays her experience through writing and drawing.

The illustration depicts her house, drawn in iconic fashion with the addition of arched windows (a Mexican architectural feature) and a snowman in the front yard (although it does not snow at all in the city where Rosa lives). Through these features of writing and illustration, Rosa has blended elements of Mexican culture, American culture, and holiday traditions to express her view of the world. These voices in Rosa's writing are words or phrases from the context of her life, the experiences she has lived through, and media she has encountered. Her cultural context includes the Spanish and English languages and the language of her generation of children.

Each student's writing will draw upon diverse voices and experiences. Examples of voices that may be found in writing along with examples of

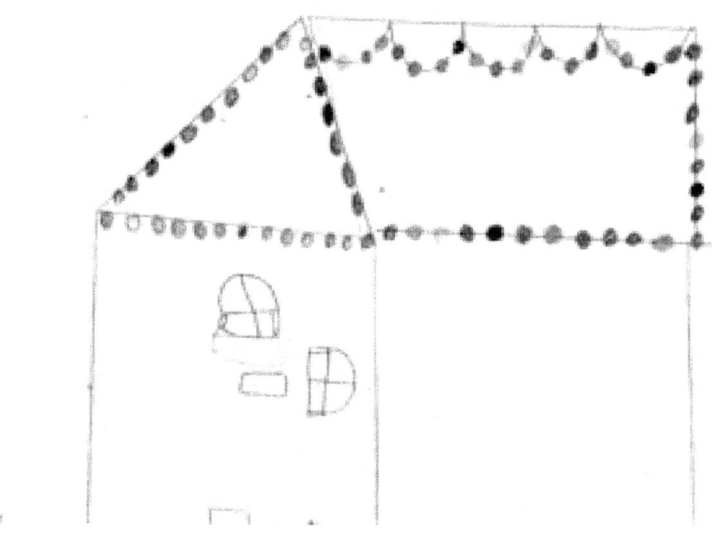

FIGURE 3.2. Illustration "My Family Tradition"

each type of voice are included in Table 3.1. The voices of family, peers, school culture, popular culture, political context, and languages are listed, with many possible sources such as video games, holidays, regional dialects, or news items. Although the table includes many examples, it is not exhaustive. There is a world of possibilities for voices when one considers that individual writers have many and varied experiences and come from numerous geographic areas. This table is only a starting point for exploring voices in student writing.

TABLE 3.1. Possible Voices in Writing.

Family Voice	Parent voice	Sibling voice	Home life	Country of origin
Writing which seems like a "performance" of another person in the family	Phrases refer to routines in the home or parental expectations such as, "I only play at home."	Refers to situations or routines in the home. Plural pronouns might indicate parents or siblings or both.	Actions that occur in the home or items found in the home such as eating dinner, getting ready for school, toys, etc.	Names of countries, states, cities, holidays, traditions, food which originates in country of origin.
Peers	**Friendships**	**Classmates**	**Groups**	
Writing that takes on the characteristics of informal "child speech" patterns	Dialogue that is written in the style of one child talking to another	Phrases and words that the class has developed as a shared vocabulary	Phrases and words that children use within affinity groups, people who have shared interests	
School Culture	**Teacher voice**	**Curriculum**	**Unit of study**	**Policy**
Writing that contains language used by the teacher or in the current classroom work	Ways of talking that the teacher reinforces through class discussions	Vocabulary and phrases related to how things are taught in the classroom such as "my reading buddy"	Vocabulary and phrases related to a particular unit of study such as "my family tradition"	Words and phrases reinforced through school policy such as "be respectful, be responsible, be productive"
Popular Culture	**TV and movies**	**Video games**	**Songs**	**Name brands**
Writing that contains slogans or words often heard in popular media	Phrases from weekly shows, cartoons, movies, commercials, public service announcements	Words, phrases, and action sequences from gaming devices	Titles, phrases and words heard on the radio, music players, television, movies, cartoons, internet, etc.	Food, clothing, games, toys, etc., such as "Bratz"

(*continues*)

TABLE 3.1. Continued

Political Events	News items	Laws	Policies	Economics
Writing that contains allusions to current or historical events	Recent or historical events which have been popularized or are significant to the community such as "9/11"	Phrases connected to laws which have become popularized such as "illegal immigrant"	School level, local, state, or national terms such as "bilingual classroom"	Words and phrases associated with local or national economic conditions such as "recession"
Languages	**Native language**	**Regional**	**Blended**	**Approximations**
Writing that contains words or phrases from the native language or a regional dialect	Spanish, Hindi, Other European Languages, Native American Languages Asian Languages African Languages, etc.	Southern English, African American Vernacular English, Mixtures of English with other languages to create unique words and phrases	The native language is blended with English at either the word level or mixed in phrases	Standard English grammar is attempted, but traces of other language or dialect linger

NOTICING LITERARY ELEMENTS AND DESCRIPTION

In addition to noticing the voices of others in student writing, we can also discover literary elements. Rosa begins her story with reasons for enjoying Christmas, quickly followed by a lovely description of the Christmas lights. She uses opposing pairs and rhyming in "lights at the night," a delightful phrase that seems to flow naturally out of her narrative.

> Christmas is a fun day because you get presents. you have to put the Christmas tree and put the presents on the tree and put the lights on the house you could see the lights at the night.

Rosa uses repetition and alliteration to reinforce the importance of decorating the house for Christmas. She tells her audience exactly what must be done to accomplish the task of decorating for the holiday: "Put the tree," "put the presents on the tree," and "put the lights on the house." She repeats the words "put the" and the word "presents"—"you get presents" and "put the presents on the tree." Repetition and rhyme highlight the importance of preparing and decorating in an orderly fashion, and we begin to anticipate what is to come as we move into the body of the narrative.

Repetition also draws attention to the fact that friends are included in the family circle because on Christmas Eve, "we all sleep and the other people sleep on our house." Although Rosa loves the lights at night, the chaos of opening presents and the dolls and gifts she receives, she is not solely focused on herself. She brings "other people" into the intimacy of this family tradition.

She writes descriptively not only about her own toys and gifts, but also those of her sisters: "and to my sister They give her a baby toy and with a *cuna* (cradle) and to my small sister a baby and a shirt it is pretty." The descriptive phrases "baby toy," "*cuna*," and "small sister" show the care and consideration Rosa gives to the happiness of others in her family. Although Rosa may not know the English word for cradle, this important detail could not be left out. Rosa used the Spanish word *cuna* in order to include her sister's gifts in the description.

We learn something very important about Rosa when we take the time to read her narrative generously. We find that along with her writing skills and her English language development, she is also developing a maturity beyond what we might expect for an 8-year-old. Rosa thinks beyond her own needs and desires to those of her family, friends, and especially her sisters. Near the end of the story, Rosa reveals herself as a responsible child who does not play with toys at school, "I only play when there's no school." The careful reader can see Rosa is a child with a sense of who she is and how to conduct herself in the world.

Literary elements and figurative language are not contrived embellishments that writers use to decorate their writing. Figurative language is something we all use every day. These elements are embedded in our language in many different ways. Rosa did not consciously decide to use alliteration in her narrative; rather, she chose words that worked to express her message and that sounded right to her. When we take the time to discover literary elements in writing, we begin to see the value, the beauty, and the labor in student writing.

Teachers of writing should be students of the literary craft by learning about metaphor, symbol, synecdoche, alliteration, and many other literary elements that have been in our language for hundreds of years. Teachers can buy books on literary elements and their uses, find them on the Internet, or simply look them up in the dictionary. Table 3.2 lays out a sample of literary elements that might be found in student writing if we take the time to look.

LOCATING THE LEARNING ZONE

Once generous reading has been completed as discussed above, Rosa's teacher can return to the form to plan instruction (Figure 3.3). In planning instruction, I want to focus on the learning zone. I need to know what Rosa is already doing well on her own because the learning zone will include what she is not yet doing, but what she can do easily with the help of a teacher or peer. I reread Rosa's narrative and the completed form to find ideas that are similar or linked in some way.

TABLE 3.2. Possible Literary Elements in Writing

Figurative Language	Metaphor	Simile	Synecdoche	Hyperbole
Expressions where words are used out of their literal meaning.	An implied comparison between two different things or ideas.	An expressed comparison of two different things or ideas.	Expressions where a part is substituted for the whole or the whole for a part.	Exaggeration for effect.
		Examples		
	It was a heavenly day.	She ran like the wind.	He longed for the comfort of the hearth.	My suitcase weighs a ton.
Other Literary Devices	**Alliteration**	**Repetition**	**Binary opposites**	**Rhyme**
	The repetition of the same first sound in a group of words.	Using a word or phrase two or more times for effect.	Opposite pairs of words.	The repetition of the ending sound in a group of words.
		Examples		
	The dark, dank dungeon.	Sarah, oh Sarah!	The lights in the night.	The lights in the night.
Other Literary Elements	**Mood**	**Theme**	**Tension**	**Telling details**
	Words and phrases used to portray feeling.	An implied or expressed topic.	A point in a story which contributes to a strained quality.	Simple, yet descriptive words that add to the mood or theme of the story.
		Examples		
	A dreary gloom pervaded our travels.	It was my best day ever.	She didn't hear the stranger's step behind her.	The little turtle was caught.

With Rosa, I find that her two biggest strengths are her descriptive detail and her strong theme. She develops detail in several different ways including using her home language, adjectives, listing the presents, and describing a scene. She develops the theme of her family's way of doing Christmas by establishing an authoritative tone, referring to her family and friends, and using unique words to reflect her family and culture.

Once I know what Rosa can do well on her own, I am ready to choose the learning zone that will move Rosa forward as a writer. Rosa is on the verge of pulling together the sections of her narrative into an organized whole.

Insights into Writing • 29

Generous Reading of "My Family Tradition"	
What voices are in this piece?	What figurative/descriptive language is in this piece?
invite other people balloon splash time to open your presents don't have time to play play when there's no school blusitas, couna (blouses, cradle)	see the lights at night see a movie in the night my bestest day ever you do a mess on your floor my bestest toy little baby toy, small sister a baby
What does it tell you about the person?	
Has a large circle of family and friend. School is an important responsibility. Loves Christmas and toys. Enjoys the chaos. She is an authority on doing Christmas. Enjoys nighttime. Cares about her sisters.	
What does this tell you about the writer?	
Uses description extensively. Uses adjectives to specify. Paints a visual picture. Uses contrast. Uses Spanish to name specific items. Uses the voice of a parent. Uses repetition to create mood. Uses unique words to reinforce the mood. Uses opposites to develop theme.	
What does this reveal about this piece?	
First part describes the setting. Second part is the action. Third part introduces conflict. Fourth part details the presents given. It is descriptive. Theme: Doing Christmas at Rosa's house. Mood: delight	
What is the student doing especially well that I want to reinforce? What can I teach that will help the student grow as a person or as a writer? What can I teach that will help improve this piece or future writing?	
Describes the scenes with detail. Has setting, action, conflict-parts of a story.	

FIGURE 3.3. Generous Reading of "My Family Tradition"

I know this because she has three parts to her narrative. The first part describes the setting, the second part contains the action, and the third part introduces conflict. These are important aspects of story writing that she has employed. The next step is for Rosa to learn how to end a narrative.

When I meet with Rosa, we sit side by side, with her narrative in front of us. I first show her where she used detail and remind her that detail is important to narrative writing. I will show her how she developed her theme and explain that all good stories have a theme. Highlighting children's strengths is highly motivating. Explicitly teaching the academic vocabulary such as "theme" reinforces their understanding of abstract concepts by connecting the concept to something tangible.

Next, I will show Rosa what she has done to organize her writing. I will point out how she organized her story with the setting, action, and conflict. Then I will ask her how she ended her story. Based upon her answer, I may follow up by showing her examples of stories that end with a strong theme statement such as the one she has in the body, "Christmas is my best day ever!"

I would give Rosa the option of adding a theme statement to the end of her piece, but would not require it. This is knowledge she can take with her into a future piece of writing. Although it is important for children to learn to revise their work, they should not be expected to mindlessly follow a teacher's suggestions. They will not learn from forced revision. Rosa can take what she learned from our conference into her future writing. An abstract concept like "theme" should be returned to at other times such as during reading and writing minilessons.

ENGLISH LANGUAGE DEVELOPMENT

Writing teachers need to know how their English learners are progressing, and analyzing their writing is one way of gaining that information. Student writing can reveal how students are making predictions about how English works based on their primary language. Language minilessons can take place during writing conferences to scaffold the student into a greater understanding of English conventions. To do this, teachers should have some knowledge or be developing an understanding of their students' primary language and an understanding of how the student is using language at their particular developmental stage.

Rosa stretched her English language ability in many ways while writing her narrative. In describing the resulting chaos inherent in unwrapping Christmas presents, "do a mess on your floor," she chose the word "do." The phrase "to do" in Spanish is *hacer*, which can mean either "to make" or "to do." By looking closely at Rosa's word choice, what at first does not sound right to a native speaker's ear—"do a mess"—can be seen as translation from one language to another. Since Rosa speaks Spanish at home and is writing about an activity that happened at home, she must translate her thoughts. In English we would say, "to make a mess," however, Rosa translated *hacer* as "to do a mess." By studying Rosa's word, I can see how she is moving between Spanish and English.

Understanding the possible translations for *hacer*, allows for a deeper understanding of both her written work and her language development. Knowing something about the student's primary language also has implications for language study. For example, we can create a T-chart with *hacer* on one side and it's translations on the other (Table 3.3).

TABLE 3.3. T-chart Language Study

We do a mess on the floor.	
hacer	to make
	to do

Language study has been used to teach English phonics, spelling, and vocabulary (Bear, Invernizzi, Templeton, & Johnson, 2012). A student's home language can also be addressed within a language-study curriculum. Some thoughts to keep in mind when thinking about helping students with language development through their writing are

- Notice and celebrate what the student is already doing well.
- Teach based upon what the student is on the verge of doing, but needs assistance with.
- Do not overload the student with too many instructional points at one time.
- Do not expect an immediate revision based on every conference or lesson.
- Notice how the student is making predictions about how English works.
- Show the student the correct English convention and compare it to their approximation.
- Notice how the student is transferring knowledge of the primary language to English.

Rosa's personal narrative about her family tradition opened a window into Rosa's life experience. Writing became an important means of communication, so she worked hard at making her writing understandable to her audience by using her knowledge of Spanish phonetics and syllabication to spell English words. Her teacher knew that linguistic knowledge in Spanish can be transferred to linguistic knowledge in English and took language diversity into account in her teaching. Knowledge of linguistic diversity is an important tool for assessing English learners' writing.

ASSESSMENT

Linguistically diverse students such as Rosa have particular strengths and needs related to their writing. When we look at such writing, we need to do more than hold it up against a model of standardized English and find the deficiencies. We need to understand the process of language development with all the complexity it entails. Rosa was concurrently developing her listening, speaking, reading, writing, and understanding of English; a very complex endeavor.

Not all assessments allow for this complexity. For instance, when her teacher focused on the analytical rubric her school district used, she described Rosa's narrative from a negative perspective.

> I noticed rambling sentences, mostly short, or sentences that are too long, really affected her sentence fluency. Her sentences are mostly incomplete, or you could say run-on; run-on sentences that had the word "and" in between. And then they are rambling and awkward. That makes the writing hard to read and understand.

By assessing Rosa's writing with a standard based on English fluency, rather than linguistic diversity, Karla focused on negative attributes as shown in the lowest rubric descriptors for sentence fluency.

> 3 - Most sentences are understandable but not very smooth.
>
> 2 - The sentences that are often choppy or rambling make much of the writing difficult to follow or read aloud.
>
> 1 - Sentences that are incomplete, rambling, or awkward make the writing hard to read and understand.

After reading the descriptions for each score with Rosa's narrative in mind, the teacher assigned Rosa a score of 1, the lowest score possible for sentence fluency. By comparing English-learner writing to a standard for native English speakers, the teacher was forced to set aside her own knowledge of Rosa's language development.

Valdés and Figuroa (1994) have written about the problems with conflating writing skill with language development and point out that many writing assessments measure the writer's ability to communicate in English as an additional language rather than the construct of writing. Assigning scores that are really a reflection of developing English does not help the student as a writer. It instead discourages the writer through the incomprehensibility of the situation. How can a student understand the way to becoming a better writer when the response is, "Your sentences are incomplete, rambling, and awkward?" What does that mean to someone in the emergent stages of learning a language?

Karla's assessment dilemma is not uncommon. State and district mandated tests are used in many schools with English learners mainly because the problem with validity is not well understood by policymakers. Teachers who work with English learners on a daily basis may understand the problem with these assessments but feel they do not have an alternative. If we cannot assess Rosa's writing accurately with this type of rubric, what can we do to understand her as a writer? If our goal is to help our students develop as writers, we must take into account who they are, and this includes the writer's cultural and linguistic background. This knowledge is essential in order to show language learners what they are doing well as writers and how they can improve.

Teachers of English to Speakers of Other Languages (TESOL) is an international organization that has developed descriptive statements of English proficiency levels (TESOL, 2006). By situating Rosa within a continuum of language development, we can see her writing as only one aspect of this. However, language proficiency levels must be seen as fluid and context dependent. Depending upon the situation and context, Rosa could be described as a level two or three:

Level 2-Emerging

At L2, students can understand phrases and short sentences. They can communicate limited information in simple everyday and routine situations by using memorized phrases, groups of words, and formulae. They can use selected simple structures correctly but still systematically produce basic errors. Students begin to use general academic vocabulary and familiar everyday expressions. Errors in writing are present that often hinder communication.

Level 3-Developing

At L3, students understand more complex speech but still may require some repetition. They use English spontaneously but may have difficulty expressing all their thoughts due to a restricted vocabulary and a limited command of language structure. Students at this level speak in simple sentences, which are comprehensible and appropriate, but which are frequently marked by grammatical errors. Proficiency in reading may vary considerably. Students are most successful constructing meaning from texts for which they have background knowledge upon which to build.

This framework helps us understand that English learners are grappling with all elements of language simultaneously. Listening comprehension, responding in a variety of situations, acquiring vocabulary, reading, grammar, spelling, and composing are all aspects of language learning that must be orchestrated in order to produce a piece of writing. Understanding language development is an essential aspect of valid assessment of linguistically diverse students.

Writing can become a window into the world of the English learner when we take the time to look closely at their voices, their literary devices, and the way in which their home language contributes to their writing. I have shown how it is possible to see Rosa's writing differently by noticing the voices and descriptive language in her writing. Voices from the contexts of students' lives, such as family experiences, media, culture, other languages, and current events, make their way into student writing, allowing us to see the student's view of the world. Literary elements such as figures of speech, alliteration, and repetition can also be found, allowing us to see the way each student uniquely crafts their writing. From this vantage point, instruction can be tailored to focus on student strengths and extend their strengths to improve both writing and English language development.

CHAPTER 4

SPEAKERS OF OTHER LANGUAGES

I born in the thailand than I have a lot tree is hot too I have mom and daddy and I have five and me if I live in Thailand I am 9. In Thailand because we do have no food My cousin tell my mom move to America and my mom move to America. Than cry becues then can Not see my fimily again than cry. I get am to apartment and then in my house. My school is good we have playground and we have room I and 4. I have a lot friend And Karen People and the bus A lot Karen people we can talk Too but do talk big.

I met Paw Htoo, a Thai-Karen girl in the beginning of her 5th-grade year. It was her second year in the United States and her first year at R.C. Bryant Elementary School. I received a class list with Paw Htoo's name, but Htoo was mistakenly listed as the family name. I later learned that Thai-Karen people do not have family names, only given names. I observed Paw Htoo during the language arts/social studies period. Paw Htoo wrote when the other children wrote, copying from books, the whiteboard, and other resources in the classroom. During breaks in instruction, she pulled a paperback book from her desk and read silently. She was focused on learning the entire time, even when there was down time and other children were playing and talking.

Student Writing: Give It a Generous Reading, pages 35–44.
Copyright © 2014 by Information Age Publishing
All rights of reproduction in any form reserved.

BEGINNING WRITING INSTRUCTION

After observing for a time, I asked Paw Htoo to come with me to a quiet spot where we could work together. I knew she lived in Thailand before coming to the United States, so I pulled an encyclopedia from the shelf and turned to the page on Thailand. Among the pictures was a photograph of a house in the mountains. Paw Htoo told me her home was similar to the photograph. After this discussion and looking at her classwork, I realized that her oral speech was developed enough for basic communication but faltered during academic discussions. Her writing consisted of seemingly random, disconnected words and phrases. I decided on a goal for our time together. I wanted Paw Htoo to write meaningful, connected prose.

I began instruction with two lined pieces of paper, one for Paw Htoo and one for me. I showed her how to fold the paper to make eight equal squares. Once she had done this, I told her I would demonstrate how to draw and write a story. I began to tell the story of how I moved from the western United States to the eastern United States. I drew a picture of the house where I grew up, with mountains and cactus setting the scene. Then I wrote under the picture, saying each word aloud as I wrote. When I finished writing, I read the completed paragraph to Paw Htoo.

"Now it's your turn to draw your home in Thailand," I said to Paw Htoo. "Did your house look like this?" I asked, pointing to the encyclopedia photo. Paw Htoo eagerly began to draw and talk about her home in Thailand. The talking, drawing, and viewing helped her articulate her thoughts and experiences. When she finished writing, she read the paragraph underneath the picture in the top left corner of the paper: "I born in the thailand than I have a lot tree is hot too." I was ecstatic! Paw Htoo had written her first bit of meaningful, connected English prose.

I moved my pencil to the next square on my paper and began drawing a picture of my family, telling Paw Htoo about them as I drew. Then I wrote under the picture, saying each word aloud as I wrote. When I finished writing, I read the completed paragraph to Paw Htoo. Then it was Paw Htoo's turn to draw and write about her family, which included her mother, father, five older brothers, and a baby sister. We continued writing in this way (Figure 4.1) with my demonstration followed by Paw Htoo drawing and writing about each step of her journey to the United States. When it was my turn to draw an airplane, I reached for an encyclopedia for ideas. Paw Htoo also drew and wrote about her airplane trip.

After we finished writing, we read our stories aloud to each other and talked some more about our lives. Paw Htoo explained that when she first moved to the United States, her family lived in a different neighborhood, with other children who spoke her language. She felt sad that her new neighborhood did not have Karen children. She missed speaking her language on the school bus.

Speakers of Other Languages • 37

FIGURE 4.1. Paw Htoo's writing

THE THAI-KAREN PEOPLE

I knew it was important to learn something more about Paw Htoo's background, so I conducted an Internet search on the Thai-Karen people and found a useful informational brochure (Karen People, 2010). I found out the Karen ethnic group lives in an area of Southeast Asia that stretches from inland Myanmar (Burma) into Thailand. Their ancestral villages are in Thailand, however now 7 million Karen live in Myanmar, and 0.5 million live in Thailand. The Karen people are culturally and linguistically diverse.

Some are Skaw Karen, Pwo Karen, or Bwe Karen. Many follow Buddhist religious traditions, while there is also a strong Christian missionary influence.

Perhaps you have heard the history of numerous human rights violations in Myanmar (Burma). Myanmar fell to military control in 1962, but a nominally civilian parliamentary government took power in 2011. That year, the human rights activist and Nobel Prize for Peace winner, Aung San Suu Kyi, was released from prison. Because of this history of persecution in Myanmar, Thai-Karen today may be indigenous to Thailand or refugees from Myanmar.

Karen refugees relocated to many places in the United States, including the southeast. I found a Karen-language Christian church not far from Paw Htoo's school. This congregation has Karen-language songbooks, the service is conducted in Karen, and the families interact socially before, during, and after the services, speaking the Karen language. On the day I visited this church, I noticed the babies quietly passed throughout the room, with many people taking responsibility for the little ones. The teenaged girls sitting behind me offered me a songbook when they noticed my attempt at singing. I read that Karen people are friendly and hospitable, and this was borne out by the warm welcome I received at the Karen Church.

It was necessary to know something about Paw Htoo's cultural and linguistic background in order to develop curriculum that was relevant to her needs. As I researched Thai-Karen, I found out that Karen value education highly. Paw Htoo's family was particularly committed to education because her father had taught adults in Thailand and her mother had taught children. After moving to the United States, Paw Htoo's father worked as a laborer and her mother cared for the baby at home.

The Karen respect teachers, and it is traditional to address teachers as "teacher." This is true of many cultures, in contrast to the United States, where we expect students to use Mr. or Ms. and the name of their teacher. In the Karen communities of Thailand and Myanmar, monks are often teachers, however some children may not receive an education because of poverty issues. Knowing that Paw Htoo's parents were both teachers, I guessed she had an education prior coming to the United States, but I was not sure of the language in which she had learned to read and write.

Because I knew Paw Htoo's background, I was able to provide resources such as library books on Thailand, written at an easy level. I chose books with beautiful photographs of modern life in Thailand so Paw Htoo could relate it to her own experience. I also gave her a large-format English picture dictionary with hundreds of words. The book was divided into sections such as classroom, kitchen, grocery store, and many other everyday settings. It also included sections for academic vocabulary encountered in school such as fairytales, space, and sports. Given Paw Htoo's interest in copying words and her concern for correct spelling, I thought she would find the book useful. Paw Htoo was happy to receive the book, and she often took it home to share with her family.

USING STUDENTS' HOME LANGUAGES

One week, I came to Paw Htoo's classroom to work with her and Victor, a Spanish speaker. The class had been studying American inventors, and they were extending their knowledge of inventions by coming up with an invention of their own. Their teacher said to think about a new, helpful device, draw it, and then describe their invention in writing. As I listened to the assignment, I was concerned that it might be incomprehensible to Paw Htoo. I wondered how to build the concepts and English vocabulary necessary for the assignment. So Paw Htoo, Victor, and I began with a discussion in English, which was our only common language. We discussed words like "invention," "machine," and "design," along with other words given as examples by their teacher and classmates. I used a piece of paper to jot down the words and drew sketches to illustrate them.

I asked what type of invention would be helpful in their lives, at home, or in school. As we talked, the children tried to express themselves, but often did not know an English word. Each time I introduced a new word, I sketched it on the paper and wrote the word beneath the picture. When the children wanted to know a word, they gestured, sketched it, and relied on their current vocabulary. Once I understood what they were getting at, I wrote the target word on the paper.

Before they began writing the assigned essay, we did a lot of talking about the concept of invention, and the children drew pictures of them. When it was time to write, I made a suggestion. They could fold their paper in half and on the left side write the essay in their home language and on the right side they could write it in English. This would help them get their ideas on paper. Victor immediately began doing this, and after three or four sentences in Spanish, he felt confident with his idea and moved to the right side of the paper, writing the essay in English.

Paw Htoo was a different matter. "I don't know how to write my language," she told me. She had never learned to read and write using the Karen language. So Paw Htoo began writing in English, using the sketches and new words for support. We continued to use the method of sketching on the scrap paper and writing the word as Paw Htoo and Victor continued. The children used the paper full of pictures and words to spell new words they needed for their writing. The children's finished essays were very satisfactory. They achieved the requirements of the assignment, showed an understanding of the concept of invention, and conveyed their ideas through English writing.

No matter what language students speak, they can begin writing as soon as they enter the classroom. Even when a teacher is not able to speak a student's language and the student is not literate in that language, accommodations can be made. Here are some of the principles I used with Paw Htoo and Victor.

- Get to know your students' cultural backgrounds.
- Provide books on your students' cultures.
- Provide books at an easy reading level with high quality photographs.
- Demonstrate writing each assignment yourself so they can see how it is done.
- Encourage them to write about their own lives.
- Talk with them about the concepts they are learning.
- Sketch and write new words for your students.
- Provide picture dictionaries.
- Encourage them to read and write in their home language.
- Make sure they have the opportunity to read their composition to someone.

Building on students' cultural backgrounds and personal experiences yields greater and quicker results than teaching and practicing isolated vocabulary and grammar. Writing meaningful, connected prose will encourage students to continue to write. Taking the time to develop concepts will allow students to express their ideas through writing.

Paw Htoo's story about moving to the United States provided a great deal of information on her life. She did not revisit this story to correct grammar or spelling, or to revise it in any way. Although it is important for English learners to eventually develop a process that includes revision and editing, they need to develop writing fluency first. By fluency, I mean the ability to write meaningful, connected prose. A generous reading of Paw Htoo's story will provide more insight than a critical editing of grammar and punctuation.

GENEROUS READING

I read Paw Htoo's story about moving to the United States using the generous reading categories of voices and literary elements. The literary element that stood out to me is "We talk too, but do talk big." This is a trope used in English but may be an element of Karen as well. Talking big may mean talking a lot—something one does with friends who speak the same language. Talking big may mean talking loudly—something children do on school buses. Or talking big may mean bragging. The use of this trope makes Paw Htoo's story interesting and makes for a strong ending. It could be used as a teaching point to show the potential meanings of "talk big" and to expand vocabulary from the word "big" to phrases such as "a lot," "constantly," or "loudly."

The voice I heard loud and clear in Paw Htoo's story was that of her cousin, as he implored Paw Htoo's mother to "move to America." This is a familiar theme in immigrant stories. Paw Htoo developed this theme through plot elements including a problem—"we do have no food"—and the solution of moving to America. Paw Htoo illustrated the complexity involved in this solution when she depicted herself crying "because then cannot see my family again."

Through generous reading, I saw some of the aspects of story Paw Htoo already controlled in her initial foray into English writing. To develop fluency, she needs many opportunities to write about meaningful events in her life. Demonstrations of such writing by supportive teachers will help her acquire the necessary vocabulary and grammar. Providing supports such as individual vocabulary work based on her current writing needs will also help her with social studies, science, and other content assignments.

MULTILINGUAL GENEROUS READING

While at a conference for bilingual educators, I was asked if generous reading could be used with other languages such as Spanish, Chinese, Arabic, Japanese, or others. There are many programs across the United States that focus on developing bilingualism. Generally speaking, these programs fall into three categories:

- Bilingual and two-way programs build on students' home languages while teaching English.
- Heritage language programs teach a language spoken in the local community, with a focus on conserving and developing languages spoken by the student or family members.
- World language immersion or two-way programs focus on teaching a new language such as Chinese or Spanish and are becoming increasingly popular at the preschool, elementary, middle, and secondary school levels.

In these programs, students will generate writing in languages other than English. In order to find out if generous reading can be used with world languages, I used generous reading with a Chinese student who recently moved to the United States with her mother, who was a graduate student at my university.

The Chinese graduate student, Xumei, was familiar with generous reading, having worked on one of my research projects. She brought her daughter's writing to my office, having already read it once (see Figure 4.1). She translated it for me, and I transcribed her words. Using my translation, I offered some of my ideas, asking Xumei if what seemed like figurative language in the translation was actually figurative language in Chinese. Sometimes the metaphor transferred across the languages and sometimes it did not. For example, "In my mind" at first sounded figurative to me, but Xumei explained that it is the normal Chinese way of saying, "I thought."

> 初至美国——开学第一天
>
> "呼～呼～！"开学了，背起新买的书包，一步一步向学校走去。刚在三周之前，我坐着飞机来到了美国，一切都跟中国有很大的差距：时间，饮食，住所以及周围的人，不得不花很大的时间，融入到新的生活中。
>
> 时间就像一滴水似的，在毫无准备的情况下流进了大海。开学，新的学校在那时的我心目中，就像一只张开血盆大口的熊，随时就要把我吞进肚子里似的，_____这就是我新学校的名字，它的吉祥物是一只马蜂。
>
> 从门口进去的那一刻起，我发现，美国的学校跟本没有那么可怕，大家友好地打着招呼，即使对我这个"外国人"也是异常欢迎，我在学校迷路时，也有人细心给我引路。
>
> 第一节课，是"英语第二语言"，专门对我这种不太懂英语的人开放。老师也是特别细心；边说着什么，边用手比划着，虽然不太明白，但我很开心，这里的老师真贴心！
>
> 最让我感动的是，上科学课时，有很多专业的用语，我什么也听不懂，老师却很关心，专门把资料打印下来，交给我，有什么实在听不懂的，助教也会再一次细心地讲给我听。
>
> 在这节课上，我还交到一个朋友，她问我来自哪里，我说是来自中国，她便跟我聊了起来，聊中国的各种食物啊，给我介绍一些美国好玩的地方什么的。
>
> 开学第一天，本来觉得那么可怕，但我现在才知道，只要你对大家友好，大家也会对你友好的。

FIGURE 4.1. Changxuan's narrative.

FIGURATIVE AND DESCRIPTIVE LANGUAGE

Sometimes a metaphor in Chinese was also a metaphor in English. Two vivid examples are, "Time is like a drop of water, it just infuses into the ocean" and "The school in my mind was like a big open, bloody mouth of a bear. It may swallow me into its stomach any time." Xumei's daughter, Changxuan, clearly understood how to use similes to express her emotions. According to Xumei, Changxuan may have appropriated the bear's mouth simile from language used in Chinese stories told to children to keep them away from danger.

Changxuan used other types of descriptive language in her narrative. She focused on the walk to school by saying, "I carried my new backpack step by step, marching to school." Step by step indicates apprehension and marching suggests steely resolve. The phrase makes it clear that the walk to school was not carefree or lighthearted.

In discussing descriptive words and phrases, Xumei pointed out the word "even," which was repeated in the narrative and served to highlight the amazement Changxuan felt that things turned out so well. "People were very friendly, even to me, this 'foreigner.'" I could picture her surprise that strangers would show her such kindness. Changxuan seemed very relieved when "I even made a new friend in my P. E. class." Again, this small word, "even," highlights the pleasant surprise of finding a friend in a new school and a new country.

VOICES

Xumei and I found several voices of others in Changxuan's writing. Since this was a personal narrative, we were not surprised to find "kid talk" in the piece. This voice is the popular language of the current generation found in children's manner of speaking. Certain sayings are common in the United States such as "Yay!" and "Oh, my gosh!" Changxuan expressed this in Chinese as 呼~ 呼~! Her use of punctuation shows the inventiveness of youth as she combines the character for "calling out" with a tilde and exclamation point.

Another voice we found in this narrative was Chinese philosophy: "I now realized that if you treat everybody friendly, you will get friendly treatment as well." Western tradition has a similar proverb, so the Chinese phrase and translation evoked similar responses from Xumei and me when we linked it to sayings we heard from our separate philosophical traditions. Another philosophical voice in the narrative—time as a drop of water—is reminiscent of Taoist sayings, which permeate Chinese language.

WHAT XUMEI LEARNED

Xumei and I were fascinated by Changxuan's writing. Generous reading revealed so much depth to the narrative that I do not have space to print everything we talked about and recorded on the generous reading form. When Xumei first read the story, she told Changxuan, "You can do better than this." However after generous reading, Xumei saw the creativity and emotion in Chanxuan's writing. She also saw that Changxuan drew upon books she had read to incorporate figurative language into her writing.

Xumei planned to use the knowledge gained from generous reading to show Changxuan how to use figurative language and descriptive detail to enhance her writing when needed. For example, a short paragraph can be augmented through descriptive detail. She also planned to use books Changxuan enjoyed reading to show how other authors use descriptive detail in their writing.

I am looking forward to continuing to use generous reading with other languages. I want to see what happens when teachers use it with English learners' writing in their home language or student writing in bilingual or two-way programs. Teachers who are multilingual can use generous reading in multiple languages, and teachers who are not fluent in their students' language can successfully use generous reading with a translator, as I did with Xumei.

This chapter began with illustrating how a beginning English learner was encouraged to write connected prose by drawing, viewing photographs, discussing, and building new vocabulary. She accomplished this by writing a narrative about her personal experience moving to the United States. A generous reading of that narrative revealed the student's use of figurative language and voices in her writing. This knowledge can be used to further develop vocabulary and story elements in future writing. The chapter closed with a generous reading of Chinese writing. This illustrated how either a bilingual teacher alone or two teachers working together can better understand a composition written in a language other than English. Generous reading led to insights into the person, the writing process, and the composition.

CHAPTER 5

LANGUAGE VARIATION

> There once was a time when a little girl went to New York. She Loved the place. She went to the water park. After that she went to the ice cream place. The Little girl name was Dimond. She went to New York the whole summer.

The 5th grader who wrote this story was an African American girl living in a small city in the southern United States. Her unique cultural background informed her writing, including content and language use.

Across the United States, students are raised in diverse settings. Some live in urban neighborhoods with people from many different cultural backgrounds. Others live in urban communities where a language such as Spanish is used at home, on billboards, and storefronts. Other students live in very small towns, where their cousins sit beside them in the cafeteria. There is not just one African American culture or one Latino culture or one Asian culture in the United States.

We often think of culture in terms of language, food, and costume, but this view is too simplistic. Culture is not static (Canagarajah, 2006a), and people often see themselves as belonging to more than one culture. They interact and connect to multiple communities in unique cultural constellations. The cultures of students will influence their writing. A former student of mine helped with the family taxi business after school, on weekends, and

---

Student Writing: Give It a Generous Reading, pages 45–53.
Copyright © 2014 by Information Age Publishing
All rights of reproduction in any form reserved.

during holidays. She had different cultural experiences than the student who spent the summer going to the waterpark and ice cream parlor in New York. The writing of both students is influenced by culture, but in distinctive ways.

We see culture through the way language is used. Language variation in student writing is a result of many different influences. Students do not speak and write in only one variety, they draw from many sources to stitch together the words and phrases needed to convey their message. Generous reading of student writing helps teachers to notice the complexity of culture and language involved in writing. Generous reading offers a more nuanced understanding of language variation than a correction-oriented perspective.

In a correction-oriented perspective, standardized varieties of English are preferred over other variations. For example, African American English is often singled out by teachers and parents for correction, yet linguists have shown that African American English is rule governed and systematic, not slang, lazy, or haphazard (Charity Hudley & Mallinson, 2011). In fact, it is seen by linguists as a language, not a dialect. Because of the increasing diversity of U.S. classrooms, it is helpful for teachers to understand African American English, Southern English, and *World Englishes*, as well as dialects of English spoken in various parts of the country.

AFRICAN AMERICAN ENGLISH

The history of African American English includes many fascinating facts and examples. Perhaps you have seen letters omitted, for example "desks" written as "des." This is one of the rule-governed forms of African American English developed as a kind of shortcut for complicated consonant clusters such as "sks." The "ks" is simply dropped to make the word easier to say.

A similar shortcut came about by dropping letters you do not hear in speech, such as the "g" in certain "ing" words. For example, "running" became "runnin." You may also notice the omission of words in sentences. Omissions developed in order to reduce redundancy. For example, "He smart." In this sentence, the meaning remains even without the word "is."

In "Diamond Goes to New York" at the beginning of this chapter, you may have noticed the missing possessive marker in the sentence, "The Little girl name was Dimond." Missing possessive markers are one feature I found in the southeastern school I studied. You may be surprised to learn that omissions such as these were a common aspect of speech in London during the late 1500s and early 1600s. This illustrates how language changes over time. There never has been and never will be a single correct way of speaking English.

Another feature of African American English is the habitual "be." In this case, the word "be" is used instead of "is." "He be goin' to school." The use of "be" implies the habitual nature of the action, in this case, going to school often, or consistently. African American English is a language with its own grammar. Some African Americans may use aspects of this grammar, while others do not. It is not a fixed aspect of culture. And I have listed only a few of the many possible features of African American English.

SOUTHERN AMERICAN ENGLISH

Some aspects of African American English are also present in Southern American English, such as omitting unvoiced letters such as the "g" in "runnin" and consonant cluster reduction in words such as "ax" for "ask." Southern American English also has unique characteristics such as the long "i" sound pronounced as "ah" in words such as "tire," pronounced "tahr." Also, the "oi" sound is often pronounced "aw" as in "bahl" for "boil." In Southern American English, you may hear "s" pronounced as "d" as in "wadn't" for "wasn't."

Students may produce unconventional spelling if their pronunciation does not match conventional spelling. The following example is an excerpt from an essay written by a European American 5th-grade student in the southeastern United States: "So we did some joy riding for a bit. After that we did go fishing. I caught like no fish so I got furious, but I cold off."

The student who wrote this worked hard on his spelling. He spelled the word "furious" correctly and erased, then corrected many words on his final paper. Yet he spelled "cooled" as "cold." This may be because he says "aw" rather than "oo" in the word "cooled." He did not catch this spelling mistake because upon proofreading, he saw that "cold" was the correct spelling for a similar word. This illustrates how important it is for writing teachers to understand that spelling mistakes are often related to the way students speak. When this is the case, it is futile to ask students to notice spelling errors only by rereading. Other strategies, such as partner editing or personal dictionaries can be used to catch spelling errors related to pronunciation.

WORLD ENGLISHES

As the global marketplace, the media, and the Internet draw us into closer interactions with people throughout the world, attention has been drawn to speakers of World Englishes in places such as the Caribbean, India, and Niger (Canagarajah, 2006b). English is also used for international trade and business dealings in countries with majority languages such as Chinese, Japanese, and German (Kachru & Smith, 2008). Along with African American English and English as a new language, writing teachers must understand the unique needs and strengths of students who grew up speaking English in a variety of countries.

English in these countries developed unique structures. You may hear variations of words such as "tire" spelled "tyre" in Britain, Australia, New Zealand, and India. Americans usually say *tie-er*, while the British and Indian pronunciation sounds like *ta-yah*. Australians might say *toe-yah*. In the Caribbean, you may hear *tie-ur* with an emphasis on *ur*. These are only some of the possible variations in pronunciation, as there are regional differences in each country.

In places where world Englishes are spoken, students are often multilingual, speaking several languages. Speaking multiple languages is a tremendous strength in a globalized world. Teachers must be aware of multiple pronunciations and spellings among English-speaking countries so student's strengths and abilities are acknowledged.

COMMUNICATIVE FLEXIBILITY

All too often, there is dissonance between the way students communicate and the demands of state standards, published curriculum, assessment materials, and the way teachers communicate. These differences can be bridged by allowing for flexibility in speaking and writing. Engagements such as reading diverse literature, engaging in conversation, performing and writing songs, and dramatic play encourage students to assimilate many kinds of language from the world around them. These activities encourage language learning based on students' sensitivity to how voices sound in various situations, and for different purposes, and participants (Dyson & Smitherman, 2009). Communicative flexibility can be encouraged with a multicultural curriculum.

Multicultural curriculum builds on the richness inherent in human experience. It should not be limited to celebrating holidays like Martin Luther King Jr. Day or *Cinco de Mayo*. It should not be limited to a unit of study on cultures of the world, focusing on food and costumes. Rather, it should be designed to uncover students' individual and cultural strengths. A writing curriculum that includes students' personal experiences in their communities, experiences with language, and family knowledge can provide many opportunities for writing that is authentic and meaningful.

A multicultural curriculum holds all students to a high standard because "all students are capable of high levels of achievement" (Nieto, 2002, p. 169). To reach this goal, students must be given access to literature that reflects their experiences. When they see themselves in literature, students are motivated to read.

Students must also have opportunities to use technology for the creation of unique products. Computers, software, and cameras are as essential in todays' world as paper and pen were in the past. For example, students might interview family or community members about an interesting topic then create a multimedia presentation based on the results. In a multicultural curriculum, students are given opportunities to ask their own questions and pose their own problems. Culturally and linguistically diverse students have important experiences that can be used as a basis for inquiry learning.

In our interconnected world, communicative flexibility is imperative. In both business and education, people from different language backgrounds must work and learn together. Students in elementary and secondary schools must develop the capacity to interact with speakers of other languages and dialects. They must also be aware of power issues, stereotypes, and prejudices connected to language (Kubota, 2004). Teachers must be aware of and confront their own perceptions.

In the United States, one standardized form of English is often valued above others. This is the variety mostly found in the midwestern states and is used by newscasters across the country. People who speak and write using standardized American English are often tacitly privileged. They may gain entry to higher education or business opportunities more easily than those who speak and write another variety.

It is often second nature to correct a child who says, "I didn't do nothin" or similar phrases. We teachers tend to react by saying, "You mean, 'I didn't do anything.'" This is called the correction method. Research has shown that the correction method is not an effective way to modify language behavior (Piestrup, 1973). It is more effective to engage students in language study that is firmly embedded in their own writing and speaking. By thinking about language used in the classroom on a metacognitive level, students gain a deeper understanding.

LANGUAGE STUDY

> I was playing video games and it had broke so we had went game stop to get a new one which my dad work there. So guest who I see is my favorite uncle Joey in the car.

In writing about her Uncle Joey, Ajia relied upon the language she grew up hearing at home, African American English. Having heard this language from the time she was born, it was a part of her. However, this piece of writing is not likely to earn a perfect score on a writing test, so it is important to help Ajia begin to think about her language. Instead of relying solely on her internalized language, she must begin to consciously think about how she uses words.

I use student writing as a basis for language study. First, I create a warm, friendly environment so students feel comfortable taking risks with their writing. Then, while the other students are writing, I pull up a chair next to someone for an individual teacher-student conference. I have the student read her piece aloud to me. I ask the student what she notices in the piece, then I tell her what I notice, focusing on the positive. Then I work on language use, focusing on only one thing. For example, with Ajia, I would say, "I'm a little confused when I hear, 'had went.' Another way of writing this sentence is, 'I was playing video games and it broke so we went to Game Stop to get a new one.' By taking out the word 'had,' it makes it easier for me to understand." I would write the revised sentence and read it to Ajia. Then I would ask her to read it. Of course, this one discussion will not be enough to cement this idea. I will have to notice how Ajia is using "had went" in future writing and possibly discuss it several times.

Another way I work on language is in whole-class discussions. When teaching the whole class using student work, I always ask the student's permission. Sometimes the student does not want to be named and other times he or she wants to stand at the front of the class and read the piece aloud. I project the writing onto a screen so the class can notice how language is used effectively and make suggestions for revision. I find the discovery method works well because students learn to notice effective language use for themselves.

I also use multicultural literature for language study. Youth novels, children's picture books, poetry anthologies, autobiographies, and many other forms of literature can be used. First and foremost, the students and I read and enjoy the literature. Students recognize their own ways of speaking when they hear the voices of published authors with the same language variation. I pull unique language from the text and talk about it during a minilesson or individual conference. Students discuss why the author used certain words or phrases and what situations are appropriate for different types of language use.

Authors use world languages and English variations for literary effect. For example, the poem, "Things" by Eloise Greenfield (2003) incorporates the phrase, "Ain't got it no more."

> Went to the corner
> Walked in the store
> Bought me some candy
> Ain't got it no more

This phrase uses the African American English double negation. (It is interesting to note that the French language also uses negatives on either side of the verb.) The repetition of "Ain't got it no more" gives Greenfield's poem voice and drives home the message that material things are fleeting. Through reading and discussing the poem, students can easily discern the theme on their own. Students will also be able to see how an African American author used language from her childhood to write compellingly from a child's point of view. Other poems by this author can be studied along with "Things" to highlight other aspects of language Greenfield used in her writing. Like Greenfield, student writers should be guided into making conscious decisions about language to suit their purpose and the mood they want to convey.

MULTICULTURAL LITERATURE

Literature engages student interests, background knowledge, and modes of learning. When students identify with characters and other aspects of stories, they can step into the story and have that vicarious experience we all enjoy. When students identify with the characters and topics, they can make predictions based on prior knowledge (Malik, 1990). They can make inferences, ask questions, and develop metacognitive awareness (Jiminez, 1997).

A language arts class full of wonderful literature is an asset to young writers. Books can be displayed face-out on narrow shelves made from plastic rain gutters or they can be kept in baskets on student tables. Students might have their own book bags, stocked with favorites to take home and share with their family. Teachers can recommend books to students during writing conferences based on the student's writing needs (Anderson, 2000). In a literature-rich environment, students will eventually recommend books to each other.

Children's and Young Adult books can be used as mentor texts (Nia, 1999) during language arts class. When teachers read books or passages aloud often, students become familiar with the sound of written language. Read aloud can be followed by lessons in which aspects of the text are examined to see how the author used language, constructed the plot, or developed characters.

Given the diversity of U.S. schools, an abundance of multicultural literature is a must for every classroom. Students need to hear voices that reflect themselves and their communities in literature (Ladson-Billings, 1995). This will help them understand the beauty of language diversity. They will understand the many genres and ways of using language available to writers. And they will gain a meta-awareness of language that will help them make decisions about which register or style to use when writing for specific purposes. They will learn what register to use when writing an emotion-filled poem and what register to use when writing a formal letter or report.

African American authors such as Langston Hughes, Ezra Jack Keats, and Christopher Paul Curtis are classroom favorites. It is wise to have books with urban, suburban, and rural characters so students can relate to the settings, but also be vicariously exposed to new experiences. I also recommend the Latina/o authors Alma Flor Ada, Carmen Lomas Garza, and Gary Soto. It is important to include specific cultures for Mexican, Puerto Rican, or other Latina/o students in your classroom. In choosing literature that reflects Asian cultures, be sure to be clear on the differences between Asian countries and cultures. To be geographically aware, students must be taught to understand the differences as well as similarities among Asian countries.

A multicultural curriculum involves more than reading multicultural literature and teaching students to use books as mentors for their writing. It involves understanding and tapping into students' cultures and experiences. The school district where I taught for 17 years adopted a practice of visiting students' homes before each new school year. The administrators, teachers, and staff formed groups, which canvassed every neighborhood, knocking on doors and speaking with everyone we met. As we walked through the neighborhoods, we reconnected with former students. We saw parents, aunts, and uncles gathered outside listening to music and talking. We saw students performing household chores and working in the family business. We noticed which parents worked the night shift and slept during the day, and which families relied on grandparents for childcare.

Luis Moll described how to build curriculum using students' home and community experiences (Moll, Amanti, Neff, & Gonzalez, 1992). One example is re-creating a home-run retail candy business in the classroom to teach economic concepts. In another classroom, Karen Cardenas-Cortez (Spence & Cardenas-Cortez, 2011) encouraged inquiry projects on social issues chosen by the students. She incorporated family library night, Internet searches, and community presentations. These are just two examples of utilizing students' home and community experiences to develop highly motivating and challenging curriculum. Each community has a unique constellation of knowledge, expertise, and culture to draw from in creating curriculum that is relevant to students and their communities.

In this chapter, I discussed the need for teachers to understand language variation. I also recommended language study within the context of student writing, suggesting some possibilities for language study, which I will briefly summarize.

- Have writing conferences with individual students. Focus on only one or two things that will help the student the most. Draw the student's attention to their language use and talk about the different ways of saying the same thing, while being respectful of the student's home language.
- Engage the class in discussions of student writing projected on a screen. Make sure you have the student's permission. Allow the student to read the piece aloud and lead a discussion of language use.
- Use multicultural literature to demonstrate the many varieties of English used in literature. Like published authors, your students can learn to use English varieties and other languages for literary effect.
- Recommend books as mentors for students. These books can be closely matched to what the students are currently writing.

These ideas are just a beginning for encouraging students to develop a metacognitive awareness of language. Remember that students have internalized the way they speak starting at birth. One minilesson or writing conference will not change how they use language. That is why it is best to focus on one thing that will help the student writer most and return to this concept frequently in many different writing contexts throughout the school year.

CHAPTER 6

WRITING ACROSS THE CURRICULUM

In today's classrooms, we expect students to read and write informational texts. Students need to understand their textbooks, and they must be able to write across the curriculum. Math, science, history, and other disciplines each have their own set of practices that students must learn to use (Shanahan & Shanahan, 2008).

Organizations such as the National Council of Teachers of Mathematics endorse using writing to help students reflect on the mathematical concepts they are learning (2006). Take a look at 5th-grade student, Ariana's, explanation of equivalent fractions to see how this works.

> Equivalent fractions are fractions that you multiply and divide. You multiply the numerator (top number) and the (denominator) bottom number) by the SAME number. You also can divide the numerator and denominator by the SAME number. Equivalent means equal to. Here are examples to help you! Problem 6/8 = 6/8 x 2/2 = 12/16 Work it out
>
>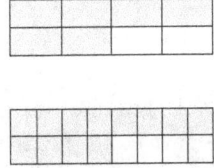

Student Writing: Give It a Generous Reading, pages 55–61.
Copyright © 2014 by Information Age Publishing
All rights of reproduction in any form reserved.

Generous reading can help us see how Ariana used elements of math writing in her explanation and how thinking and writing reinforced her understanding of equivalent fractions. In generous reading, we pay attention to the voices we hear in writing. One can clearly hear the voice of a math teacher or textbook in the phrases, "Work it out" and "Here are examples to help you!" The voice of a textbook is also evident in the explanation within parentheses, "numerator (top number)" and clear pictures that illustrate the concept. Ariana seemed to be emulating math textbook writing, which, by 5th grade, she knew quite well.

Generous reading also involves noticing literary elements and descriptions. Ariana's description, "fractions that you multiply and divide" showed that she understood the purpose for using equivalent fractions. Her statement made sense because if the fractions are not equivalent, you cannot multiply and divide them.

Ariana's teacher, Joyce, expected her students to write in order to develop their conceptual understandings. She also knew that writing would be required in high school and college classes. She knew that mathematicians write as part of their work. People who use mathematics in their careers write project reports or articulate complex ideas for an audience of their peers (Russek, 1998).

Joyce also understood that writing is a useful assessment tool. When she used generous reading, Joyce decided to think about what it told her about Ariana as a mathematician. This is what she learned: A mathematician must be very detailed in her work, and Ariana provided the necessary detail through her descriptions and illustrations. Joyce knew that mathematicians must be fluent in multiple modes of expression, and Ariana expressed the concept through words, numbers, and illustrations.

Joyce also learned something about Ariana as a writer. Ariana wrote for an audience of other students, used mathematical language such as "equal to," and wrote clear, detailed explanations. The writing itself was descriptive, organized, and had a clear purpose.

After thinking about the mathematician, her writing process, and the math writing itself, Joyce used generous reading to think about the type of instruction that would further develop Ariana's math writing. While Araina's writing was strong, the use of generous reading helped Joyce to think about how it could be improved.

Ariana was able to draw on the voice of the textbook, but she did not give any concrete examples. Other students in the class gave examples from their experiences, such as counting coins or doubling a recipe. Using a concrete example to illustrate the mathematical concept would make her writing stronger and more engaging. It would show that Ariana is capable of connecting abstract concepts with her own experiences. After Joyce used generous reading to analyze Ariana's writing, she planned to encourage Ariana to think of concrete examples to add to her writing.

GENEROUS READING OF SCIENCE WRITING

Like mathematicians, scientists must write in a variety of forms including, "personal notes, memos, diagrams, graphs, grant proposals, and reports." (Yore et al., 2004, p. 349). Like math, writing can be used in science class to develop understanding, assess what students have learned, and develop the type of writing used by scientists. Science texts are full of difficult vocabulary. One aspect of science vocabulary is the tendency to create nouns out of verbs. For example, instead of saying, "I mixed the ingredients" a science text might say, "A mixture of ingredients." Science texts are often difficult for students because of the unique vocabulary.

Joyce also taught science. Her goal for science writing was for students to use scientific vocabulary learned over the course of the semester. In December, she assigned an informal writing exercise using vocabulary and content knowledge to write a letter to a friend explaining how to eat healthy snacks. One student, Reed, wrote about making such snacks.

> We are making you a healthy trail mix. You should start by drinking a healthy solution like hot choco or coffie, and if you get hungry you should try eating a healthy mixture like dried mangos, raisens, nuts, goldfish, and pretzals. If you want to make the coco your self then put coco in milk but make sure the coco is the solute and the milk the solvent. When you buy the coco powder make sure it is fat free. If you buy the coco poder then the coco poder should be 45% and the milk or water 55%. The concentration should be good because the coco shouldn't be to thick

Joyce used generous reading to look closely at Reed's science writing. The voices in the writing came from American consumer culture, with a focus on contents of prepared foods. The phrase, "fat free" and repetition of "healthy" show that Reed had been exposed to these terms, probably in the grocery store and on television. He also used the voice of one child speaking to another in the phrases, "if you get hungry" and "if you want to make the coco yourself." One literary element was repetition, "healthy trail mix," "healthy solution." He also repeated "make sure."

The phrases "Make sure the coco is the solution" and "make sure it is fat free" convey a tone of authority. His authoritative tone suggests Reed believed eating healthy is important. He used scientific vocabulary in his descriptions of the hot cocoa and trail mix, contributing to the authoritative tone.

Joyce noticed that Reed was actively learning about writing by trying out scientific vocabulary. He experimented with word "solution" using the Latin root "solut" rather than the more common "dissolve." He successfully used commas for listing items and commas within a complex sentence. The one thing Joyce felt Reed could improve was elaboration. She wanted him to develop his topic through descriptive language.

Joyce, like many teachers today, wanted to prepare her students for possible careers in science, technology, and math. She wanted to develop skills that would help in high school and college courses that would lead to careers in math and science. Writing is an essential component of this preparation. She realized that making science fun, connecting it to the real world, and giving students many opportunities to use and write about science was essential. At the same time, the traditional training many teachers received in their youth make them hypervigilant correctors of mistakes. Over correcting student work saps the fun, creativity, and motivation from even the liveliest lessons. Generous reading helped Joyce see the positive attributes of writing first and think about instruction in a new light.

HISTORY WRITING

Historians work with both fact and interpretation. Students in school have traditionally only dealt with facts, consuming the products of professional historians through reading, memorizing, and taking tests. However, recent teaching practices encourage students to engage with history like real historians. This means students must compare and contrast different sources, including primary sources. Students must understand that historians take a position through their writing. Students must also construct their own interpretations based on evidence (VanSledright, 2002).

A 5th-grade teacher, Diane engaged her students in a process similar to historians. In teaching a unit on child labor during the Industrial Revolution, she used the photography of Lewis Hines, who was an investigative photographer for the National Child Labor Committee from 1908 to 1912. These photographs depict children working as newsboys, textile mill workers, miners, factory workers, and in many other jobs. Diane used posters of the photographs, video clips, and a flipchart of information to prompt class discussions. After engaging with this content for about a week, students each picked one photograph and used it as inspiration to write a historical fiction account in first person. Michael wrote from the point of view of a newsboy.

> I've been working as a news boy. We moved here from France. I'm 11 years old. My brothers name is Dustin. We're both news boys. We don't have a mom. My mother died of a heart attack. We have a dad he's sick. He coughs and every time he coughs, it's black. We know that he's dying young. On Sundays we all pray together just for a raise or just for better working conditions. When we don't play with friends we go relax or sleep for the work ahead of us. I'm still not lonely. We all thought that this was the land of dreams The sad thing

is we all live in a one story shack with barely enough money to feed us. One day I found a stray cat and named him Bob.

In this historical fiction piece, Michael took on the persona of a newsboy whose mother was already dead and whose father was dying from lung disease related to working as a coal miner. Coal miners were often afflicted with lung disease from breathing coal dust, and sanitary conditions were deplorable in the ghettos of this era, causing high mortality rates. Michael used these historical facts to depict an immigrant family by combining information from various aspects of the unit of study on the Industrial Revolution. Diane noticed Michael's use of figurative language, calling America "the land of dreams." She was impressed that Michael would use this phrase and thought he may have heard it in the videos they watched during class. Diane also noted figurative language in "we go relax, or sleep for the work ahead of us." She thought the phrase, "work ahead of us" aptly portrayed the fact that children did not really experience childhood during this time period, due to their work responsibilities.

Diane had very clear views on how to teach history in fifth grade. She did not use a textbook because she felt the information was too dry and "cold" for students, making it difficult to comprehend. She said that history is a "hard subject to convey if you don't make it somewhat personalized." She delivered content through photographs, posters, videos, and flipcharts instead of the textbook. To Diane, the visual nature of her instruction was instrumental in Michael's understanding.

Diane described how generous reading revealed something of Michael as a student. She said, "Well I think he absorbs what is taught. He internalizes it and I think sort of processes it." Diane believed the writing assignment helped Michael understand and process what he learned about child labor saying, "What better way to comprehend the information than to take a little trip in his shoes."

Writing historical fiction in first person allowed Michael to take in historical facts delivered mainly through visual modes and to produce a piece of writing that displayed his knowledge of social issues and living conditions during the Industrial Revolution. The social studies require an understanding of abstract concepts such as belief systems, change, empathy, and identity. These cannot be learned directly through memorization of facts. They require immersion in ideas, time to reflect, and engagement through reading, writing, speaking, listening, and doing. Through the visual and auditory modes used for Diane's instruction, and a writing assignment that required empathy and deep understanding, Michael was able to grasp some of these important abstract social studies concepts.

IDEAS FOR INSTRUCTION

The teachers in this chapter integrated writing with the content areas of math, science, and social studies. Writing across the curriculum is essential for preparing students for their futures and for developing a deep understanding of abstract concepts in the content areas. The National Commission on Writing (2003) calls attention to the importance of writing in learning.

> If students are to make knowledge their own, they must struggle with the details, wrestle with the facts and rework raw information and dimly understood concepts into language they can communicate to someone else. In short, if students are to learn, they must write. (p. 9)

Writing to learn in math, science, and history means students will use writing as a tool to develop their understanding. We can expect to see approximations toward deep understanding in their writing. Building on what their writing reveals, we can use that to move students forward in their thinking. Generous reading of math, science, and social studies writing allows teachers to see a student's current understandings rather than expecting a fully formed understanding. Generous reading reveals the learning process. Here are some ideas for content area writing.

- Math and Science Journals—Journals are a record of student's growing understanding of concepts. Children from as early as kindergarten and throughout the upper grades can create journals according to their ability. They can include pictures, cut and pasted artifacts, descriptions, observations, procedures, and results. The journals can be as sophisticated as necessary for grade-level expectations. Students can use headings, tables of contents, and other text features to make information easy to find and to reflect on their own learning.
- Multimodal Writing—Think of writing as multimodal and include opportunities for students to learn and express their understanding through illustrations, photographs, videos, tables, graphs, speaking, presenting, and audio recordings.
- Collect Resources—Primary sources such as realia, artifacts, and field trips are vital for historians and should be included in the curriculum whenever possible. Math and science concepts can be explored through field trips, instruments, organisms, specimens, and models.
- Literature—Use children's and young adult literature to explore how authors write about history, science, and math.
- Displays—Use environmental print, posters, bulletin boards, and photographs for visual reinforcement of abstract concepts and as resources for writing.

- Graphic organizers—Teach students to use graphic organizers to group ideas, to classify, organize information, and find patterns.
- Big Ideas—Integrate the curriculum by starting out with a concept that will connect ideas presented across content areas and that will link units of study. Use generous reading to uncover the ways in which students refer to the big ideas in their writing.
- Sharing and Discussing—Encourage whole-class sharing and discussion so students can learn from one another's strengths. Project student writing onto a screen for the whole class to see. Have the student read their writing aloud and encourage positive comments from the class. Use information from generous reading to highlight aspects of the writing from which other students can learn.

CHAPTER 7

TEACHERS WORKING TOGETHER

After the school day was over, four teachers sat around a large classroom table with me. We were reading a fictional story written by Ricky, a fifth grader. Step into the classroom with me and listen.

Lucy:	Did everybody finish? Okay, remember that voices are just things that kids hear every day around them in the world—on TV and radio, from the teacher, their family. What voices do you hear in this?
Toni:	I think TV and things like that.
Lucy:	Oh, "Rascal's going to be devious and destroy the tree." Yeah, it almost sounds like a . . .
Toni:	Cartoon or video game or something.
Nancy:	And the dialogue down at the bottom, "I've gotcha!" and "I'm okay."
Lucy:	You can fill this out for Ricky, your student and we can just help you by talking about it.
Beth:	You use onomatopoeia in your class a lot, so it's got the "crack," the "Aaaa!"

Student Writing: Give It a Generous Reading, pages 63–69.
Copyright © 2014 by Information Age Publishing
All rights of reproduction in any form reserved.

Lucy:	So you think it has the voice of the classroom, kind of?
Toni:	Definitely.
Lucy:	So put that, for voice. Voice of the classroom, "crack," "Aaaa." Sometimes I put where the voice comes from as well as one of the words or a phrase to help me remember.

Toni began to fill out the generous reading form, while the rest of us reread Ricky's story with new understanding. We could now visualize Rascal as a cartoon character, and we knew that Ricky had learned about onomatopoeia. Onomatopoeia means words that sound like the thing they reference.

Voices from television and cartoons are likely to show up in children's writing, since children in the United States watch an average of three to four hours of television a day (AACAP, 2011). Toni noticed the cartoon-like quality of the writing but was also relieved to know that classroom instruction had an equal impact. In fact, Ricky was able to use his knowledge of cartoons to put Toni's lesson on onomatopoeia to good use.

I met with these four teachers three times during the school year. Each time, they brought samples of their student writing, which we discussed together. Sometimes they had already filled out generous reading forms, and other times they wrote on the forms as we talked. Each piece of writing was fascinating in its own way and was filled with nuances that the five of us collaborated to find. It was extremely helpful to think together about each piece of writing because generous reading was new to these four teachers. They had previously used analytical rubrics to evaluate student writing, but they had never used sociocultural and literary analysis.

The four teachers found that working together helped them think about individual writers, such as Denise, who had moved from Mexico the previous year. Her teacher, Nancy, told us about her concerns.

Nancy:	And I chose her for a reason, because, I mean, she's relatively new to this country. She came here a year or so ago. She's a very bright student and has made tons of progress. But her writing is an area of concern for me.

English learners who enter U.S. schools in the upper elementary grades have literacy skills from their native language that transfer to English writing. However, some literacy skills do not directly transfer, such as Spanish and English sentence structure. These students produce an interesting mixture of sophisticated concepts and uneven grammar. Discussing this English learner's writing with a group of teachers, including an ESOL-certified teacher, helped Nancy see it from a different perspective.

Assessing student writing with other teachers is the best way to learn any assessment tool. However, generous reading is very different from typical writing assessments because the focus is on understanding the writer and the writing process, as well as analyzing the actual story or essay. It requires seeing the writing in a different way—looking beyond surface mistakes. It requires thinking deeply about the student's identity. Teachers must retrieve their knowledge of literary analysis, which for some has not been used since college.

HELPING EACH OTHER LOOK BEYOND

Rachel wrote this essay:

> I am most grateful for having a family that loves and supports me, teacher, and food and water without this my life would not be complete. The first thing i am grateful for is having a family that loves and supports because no matter what i do right or wrong they still love me. Without my family I would be nobody in this world. I would be sad without them.

Sometimes it is difficult to see your own students' writing objectively. We can all relate to how Toni, Rachel's teacher, felt when we started reading Rachel's essay.

Lucy:	What are some of the voices you heard?
Toni:	Oh, my gosh! How do you not capitalize "I"?

Working as a group, when Toni couldn't get beyond the surface mistakes, we were there to help her notice voices in the writing.

Lucy:	You know—I see this, "My life would not be complete." How many times have you heard that? I wonder where she heard it? Do you have any idea?
Toni:	Mom.
Lillian:	If she watches the novelas [Spanish language TV dramas], she might have gotten it from that because if she's a fifth grader, she's probably watching the novelas.
Doris:	Maybe church.

We went on to talk about how the words Rachel chose revealed something about the experiences and influences in her life. By understanding Rachel as a person, Toni was able to think about instruction that would have a deeper impact. In contrast, reminding her to capitalize "I" is something that takes two seconds and does little to develop the writer.

After discussing many more aspects of this essay, Toni decided to focus on the second paragraph, developing the theme of family.

Lucy: So would you have her revise this piece or would you teach her something about this piece that she could go and do next time?

Toni: I might take this and use it as a springboard and say, "Tell me about your family," and if she has sisters, for instance, I would have her write a paragraph on each one. These are my siblings. And each sister gets their own paragraph. I want to know who she is: Is she older? Is she younger? Do you play with her? Do you fight with her? Zooming in on this one piece of it and expanding it.

Through generous reading, Toni noticed the vivid language Rachel used in writing about her family and decided to use that as a springboard for another piece of writing that would build on this capacity for writing compellingly.

SHARING IDEAS FOR INSTRUCTION

Lillian participated in our after-school generous reading group, even though she taught at another nearby school in the district. She was eager to learn about generous reading in order to meet the needs of her English learners. Lillian noticed how Ivan, whose family came from Argentina, grew as a writer.

Lillian assigned the writing prompt, "If you could be rich or famous, which one would you be and why." The small group of English learners in her class discussed possibilities, and they each planned their writing with a graphic organizer. Then Ivan wrote a paragraph about what he would do as a famous soccer player.

> Rich or Famous If I could become rich or famous I would want to be famous. I would want to be a FAMOUS SOCCER PLAYER I played it since I was born. My family always watches the world cup on TV. My Grandpa was in the world cup and won once. His team was Argentina. Teaching little kids to train with us would be my goal.

The teachers each had a copy of Ivan's writing. They read it silently, then began to talk about the voices they noticed, which were family tradition, TV sports announcing, and the school's P. E. teacher. They talked about the literary elements such as hyperbole—"I played it since I was born." Hyperbole is exaggeration for effect, and you can see how Ivan exaggerated how long he had been playing soccer.

When the teachers were ready to talk about Ivan's writing process, Lillian had some definite ideas about his development over the semester and what she planned to teach him next. The other teachers helped Lillian think about her ideas for instruction.

Lucy:	Does noticing any of this—the voices or the special uses of language—teach you something about him as a writer?
Lillian:	I know that he has matured a lot from the beginning of the school year because a lot of the minilessons that I have given them have been on sentence variation. I can see that he's taken some of my minilessons on sentence variation and used them because in the beginning, everything would start with "I." He's still got a lot of "I"s in there, but that last sentence, "Teaching little kids to train with us would be my goal." He would not have done that before.
Nancy:	Yeah, that's a great sentence.

Although it is not a perfect sentence, "Teaching little kids to train with us would be my goal" was a different construction than Ivan usually produced. He was moving from starting sentences with "I" to experimenting with different types of sentences. Lillian saw that as a significant step forward. Ivan was not only thinking about getting his ideas on paper, but also how to write interesting sentences.

Lillian planned to use this piece of writing to teach Ivan how to separate his ideas into several paragraphs and add more details to develop them. The teachers brainstormed ways to accomplish this. Doris suggested he write one paragraph describing the family as they watched soccer on TV. Another paragraph could provide more detail about the grandfather's World Cup experience. The final paragraph could tell why Ivan wanted to use his position as a famous athlete to work with little kids.

LETTING GO OF WHAT WE KNOW

In the three times they met across one school year, this group of teachers gave one another new perspectives on teaching. They openly shared their ideas, successes, and questions about teaching writing. One of the most valuable aspects of these discussions was reading student writing from other classrooms.

Nancy:	I found it actually easier to read yours than my own. I found it more beneficial here with someone else's, not having the preconceived notion of who that student is. I'm harder on my own student than I am with someone else's.
Doris:	It's hard to separate what we know about the student with what they write. You might say, "That is a great story." And I think, "Well, you could have done better," because I've seen what he knows. When you said, "I loved what he did there," I didn't see it because I know the child. When we

didn't know the child whose work we were reading, the blind evaluations among us gave us a fresher view.

Perhaps sharing the writing of other students is a good first step in learning generous reading. The teachers found it much easier to be generous with student writing when they were not responsible for teaching that child. Not knowing the writer, they could focus on how the writer used voices of others, literary elements, and descriptive language to communicate ideas. They could speculate on what the writing says about the person and their writing process. They could read the writing expecting to learn something. They could let the writing affect them emotionally, as when Doris responded to Ivan's writing, "I think I can see him watching the world cup and saying, 'Granddaddy, you did that and you were there. Tell us about it.'"

LESSONS LEARNED

Generous reading with a group of teachers provided opportunities to see writing differently. The teachers thought about how students were progressing as writers, and they brainstormed ideas for instruction. At first, it was difficult to think about their own students' writing objectively, but after reading many students' writing over the course of a year, the teachers saw the benefits of this new perspective. By the end of the year, even Toni, who tended to be quite critical with her students' writing, was able to find a use for generous reading. For example, Toni highlighted creative language as we discussed her student, Amber's, story.

Lucy:	And so if you took this to her again because you wanted her to expand on it, what would you tell her that she was doing really well?
Toni:	Her voice. I think her voice is very good. I like the expression. There's a sense of visualizing, you know, "shimmering, glimmering shoes," "slip-on shoes." She's specific with that language.

Lillian, the ESOL teacher, found that generous reading helped her think through ideas for teaching.

Lillian:	These last two questions on the form helped me a lot: "What can I teach that will help the student grow as a person or as a writer?" I began to think a lot more about that after conferencing with them. And, "What can I teach that will improve this piece or future writing? It also helped me to see what they all had in common in the class. There was a lot of commonality that I extracted from that. And I

don't think I've looked at that before. So those two questions are going to help to drive what I'm going to do for another year.

Generous reading helped Lillian think deeply about her students as writers. Additionally, she could see their commonalities after having thought about each of her students in this way. She could see that they were often drawing on some of the same voices in their world. She could see how they were using language. Through these insights, Lillian developed a clear idea of how to help them develop as writers based on these shared attributes. Lillian saw generous reading not just as a way of individualizing instruction, but as a way of finding common aspects of writing in a classroom of students.

Generous reading with a group helped teachers get past what they perceived the student should be able to do. They were able to begin seeing student writing as a reflection of voices and experiences in the child's world. They generated ideas for individualized instruction as well as commonalities among students that could lead to whole-class writing lessons. Lillian gained new insights into her English learner's writing that she planned to use for instruction in the upcoming school year. Based on these teachers' experiences, I highly recommend trying generous reading with a group of teachers and their students' writing.

CHAPTER 8

CUTURALLY RELEVANT INSTRUCTION

> Have you ever made a wish? I have. It would be that my dad and my sister could come back. Well my Dad is at Uraguay and my sister is in Spain. Nicholina's real name is Araceli, but I call her Niki. I got the name Martina from my dad Martin. Just add a a to Martin and it would be my name. I love both of them. Nicholina left because her boyfriend. She loved him so much that she left. My dad wouldn't tell me why he left. I thought they'll never leave me but they had to. If they come back I'll go everywhere with them even to Disney World. I told you what my wish is. I hope it comes true one day!

Martina, the 4th-grade author of this narrative, was bilingual. She spoke both Spanish and English and received English instruction in a biweekly class with another girl and four boys.

Martina's story clearly shows the international flavor of a family. Martina was born in the United States, but currently has a father in Uruguay and a sister in Spain, just like the fictional characters in her story. Her teacher used fiction writing as an opportunity for Martina to express her feelings, which provided purpose and motivation as she wrote this piece. Her teacher understood that culturally relevant instruction builds on students' cultural backgrounds to help them achieve academically (Ladson-Billings, 1995).

Goals of culturally relevant instruction are compatible with generous reading. In both, personal experiences are valued. Generous reading requires thinking about students as people who are developing individual and social identities. Martina's narrative highlights this struggle for identity within a family unit. The phrase, "I thought they'll never leave me but they had to" implies the question, "Am I loved?" This is an important question for a girl who is quickly growing up. She has an older sister who already left home to follow a boyfriend. Martina ponders this action in relation to her own identity.

Culturally relevant instruction requires thinking about student writing as embedded in the social realities of their world and can lead to developing critical perspectives (Ladson-Billings, 1995). Students develop decision-making and social action skills through writing. Generous reading helps them learn that their words come from the world around them and can influence others. In Martina's story, the phrase, "She loved him so much that she left" seems to come from a *novela*, soap opera, or romance novel. Pointing this out to Martina would help her to see that she is drawing on ideas from literature or television to write and think about her own identity as a girl who is growing up. In the process, Martina can learn to critique literature that depicts romance as the road to happiness.

PERSONAL HISTORY

Using personal history as a resource as Martina did is one aspect of culturally relevant instruction. Student culture, language, and experiences can form the basis for academic success. Martina's teacher created conditions for academic success through a workshop environment. She used posters to illustrate punctuation rules, parts of a story, and to suggest opening lines. She reviewed these with the whole class and referred to them often during the writing workshop. She also reserved time to sit next to each student to discuss individual work.

Another way to provide culturally relevant instruction is to use cultural motifs. These are dominant ideas within a culture, for example, Latina/o cultural values of *familia* (Nieto, 2009). Martina's teacher understood that family is an important topic for writing. She encouraged another student with Uruguayan parents as he wrote about soccer, an important sport in that country. The boy's dream was to coach soccer, emulating his grandfather who played for Team Argentina at one time (see Chapter 7). Classrooms that include personal histories and cultural motifs have a sense of support and caring. The teacher is seen as a family member or friend. The family relationship can build academic success because in many Latina/o families, students work hard in school to make their families proud. Students in Martina's class demonstrated this sense of family by helping each other with ideas for their writing. They provided each other with positive feedback and suggestions for improvement.

THE AFFECTIVE FILTER

For students who are beginning to learn English, we must lower the affective filter (Krashen, 1987, 1988). Affective refers to emotion and feelings. Filter refers to a blockage that does not allow learning to take place. The lower the level of anxiety, the easier it is to acquire a new language. The learning environment should be comforting and nurturing, yet challenging. Tests and quizzes are stressful for all learners and particularly for English learners. Alternative evaluations should be used whenever possible. Students can be given choices of how to respond. Drawing, simple yes and no, or using their home language are possibilities. And always allow sufficient wait time to let students think about how to respond in English.

A nurturing classroom can also gently push students to reach their potentials. Even English learners can participate in oral presentations in small groups. Groups of students can also create skits, songs, and games that relate to the content they are learning. Celebrations with parents and other family members can be planned after completing a unit of study. Students will learn more about one another and will come together as a community.

VALUING LANGUAGES

Another way to be culturally responsive is to treat native language ability as an advantage. Some schools do this through bilingual education programs, world language instruction, or heritage language programs. Encourage students to continue to study their native language even if the school does not officially support it.

Validate linguistically diverse students in the classroom and express an interest in what they have to say. Provide bilingual books, books containing African American English, or books written in other varieties of English. These books show students their language is valued in society and can be used in writing. Learn to pronounce the names of students correctly and use their names often. Learn about the educational and family background of students. Ask parents and family members to provide recipes, songs, product labels, newspapers, magazines, and other resources in their home language.

LANGUAGE STUDY

A culturally responsive approach values and appreciates the richness inherent in language variation (Charity Hudley, & Mallinson, 2011). The English language varies across the United States and is continuously changing.

For example, "Ya'll" and "you guys" have left their southern and eastern regions and have spread across the United States. New innovations in language such as "LOL" for "Laugh out loud" have been introduced through texting and tweeting electronic messages. Teach students about language variation so they will know in which settings to use the different phrases. Brainstorm situations in which the students would use familiar variations versus standardized English.

Generous reading can help you find and discuss special phrases students use. In the south, I have found phrases such as "wondering on," "a good amount," and "I'm just saying," among many interesting expressions common in this region. Students use regional expressions because they grew up hearing them, but talking about such expressions within a linguistically diverse classroom helps students think about how they use language in relation to how other people, including their classmates, use language. Just because we say things differently does not mean someone is wrong.

Correcting students' English without explaining why only leads to more errors (Piestrup, 1973), yet we can agree that students must learn to speak standardized English when necessary. One of the variations of standardized English is "school English"—language that school personnel and students use to describe their activities at school. School English will vary from school to school. For example, I heard teachers refer to "writers notebooks," "journals," and "interactive notebooks." These were all used for writing on an ongoing basis.

Another variation of standardized English is "academic English." Academic English is important for entry into many opportunities in our society, therefore it is a necessary component of instruction. Martina's teacher developed academic language in a group discussion during writing workshop. She was speaking with Martina when she asked the rest of the class for ideas to help Martina with the beginning of her story.

Teacher:	Remember we talked about beginnings? How can we start stories?
Martina:	Umm.
Student 1:	[Pointing at the wall.] We can use one of those words.
Student 2:	Like, ask a question.
Teacher:	Ask a question. Or make it mysterious.
Student 3:	Exciting.
Teacher:	Make it exciting so someone will want to read it.
Student 2:	Persuasive?
Teacher:	If it is persuasive writing, but in her case, she's writing fiction.
Student 2:	A wish. Have you ever made a wish before?
Martina:	Yeah.

The students had created a list of possible ways to begin a story, which hung on the classroom wall. They referred to this list during the discussion. The teacher used academic language related to writing such as "beginnings" and "mysterious." She referred to academic concepts such as "persuasive writing" and "fiction."

Writing workshops and other constructivist teaching methods are effective for teaching academic language. Students construct their knowledge of academic English by using it for authentic purposes related to their lives. In contrast, a transmission model of instruction assumes the teacher must give information to students, who lack knowledge. The constructivist model is more effective because all students have cultural and linguistic knowledge to use as a foundation for learning.

It is essential to resist the urge to simplify vocabulary and content. Teachers and students must use academic vocabulary every day. You can use academic word walls to refer to during instruction and acknowledge when the words are used. Let students in on the secret—that academic language is a key to unlocking doors of opportunity. It is the key to your students' futures.

TEACHING GRAMMAR

While teaching academic English is important, it is acquired gradually, over time. So we should not hold students accountable for perfection. In Martina's story, she wrote, "My sister left because her boyfriend." What is really wrong with this sentence? Not much. If we simply add the preposition "of," it will sound right. "My sister left because of her boyfriend." Prepositions are difficult for English learners and take time to master. Martina's teacher did not focus on small grammatical mistakes because the story was focused, organized, and had a good introduction and ending.

Mention the word "grammar" to anyone and you will likely receive a negative reaction. Yet there is no doubt that grammar as a system underlies every language and allows us to communicate meaningfully. When teaching grammar, keep in mind the basic tenets of culturally responsive instruction. Create an atmosphere in which students feel they can take risks in their speaking and writing. Incorporate students' experiences, culture, and languages into your teaching. In this type of environment, grammar instruction will enhance student writing (Weaver, 2008).

Grammar instruction must be consistent as students progress through the grades. Standards for instruction address the skills that should be developed and reinforced at each grade level. Too often we want student writing to be grammatically perfect, without giving it time to develop. For example, an instructional standard for fourth grade includes, "form and use prepositional phrases." Martina, a 4th-grade English learner, wrote, "Well my dad is at Uruguay and my sister is in Spain." She is able to form correct prepositional phrases—"is in Spain"—but has not developed an ear for which preposition sounds right—"is at Uruguay." This is tricky for English learners because the preposition "at" is often used with a location, for example, "at home."

One way to approach teaching grammar is to demonstrate the skill to students using your own writing, phrases from books the class has read, or student writing. Use the whiteboard, chalkboard, or projection technology so the whole class can discuss the skill. You may underline or highlight different types of prepositional phrases in a variety of sentences. Students will relate best to phrases they currently use such as, "at home," "in Spain," "on the bus," before he left," "after school."

Once you have demonstrated the skill, students can work in groups or on their own to find examples of prepositional phrases in their own writing. They can also look in children's and young adult literature for ways authors use prepositional phrases to enhance their writing. Once they are familiar with noticing and discussing the grammatical form, they should have opportunities to use it in their own, purposeful writing. These instructional steps can be used for any grammar skill:

- Find out the grammar standards for the grade level you teach.
- Notice the grammar skills your students are using, beginning to use, or are not using yet.
- Demonstrate a grammar skill expected for the grade level.
- Ask students to find the grammatical form in their own writing or books.
- Provide opportunities for students to use the grammatical form in their own writing. Do not assign sentences just to practice the skill. Purposeful writing could be writing about their experiences in a writer's notebook or journal.

ASSESSMENT AND GRADING

We must make sure our grading policies for writing are fair to linguistically diverse learners. My suggestion is to grade grammar separately, so students can see their progress over time. A separate grade for content will show how well the student understands the content. In Martina's case, the content of instruction was writing an organized story. Therefore, her grade should depend on how well she organized the story, not her English proficiency. Provide information so that students, parents, and caregivers are aware of how grades are determined and what they are measuring. A student, parent, or caregiver who sees a grade of A, B, C, or 1, 2, 3 or 6, 5, 4 often does not know what the student did to earn the grade or what they need to do to improve their grade. Instead, some type of explanation should accompany any grade, as in this example for Martina (Table 8.1).

A letter or numerical grade is a quick way to rank students and to compare them with other students in the classroom, but it is not very useful

TABLE 8.1. Martina's Writing Grades

Grade	Skill	Description
A	Organizing a story	Her story focused on one topic. It had an introduction and an ending.
B	Grammar- prepositional phrases	Correct use of "in Spain" Need more practice using "at" and "of."

information for the student, parent, or caregiver. A grading system that includes the instructional goals and description of how the student met, partially met, or needs to meet the goal provides specifics that can be acted upon.

A culturally responsive approach to instruction considers who the student is as a person and how they are developing their identity. It builds upon cultural motifs such as the value of families. Developing a family atmosphere helps keep anxiety to a minimum, and community and family members can contribute their expertise to the classroom.

To create culturally responsive instruction, value all languages and use them as instructional resources, accepting English language variation as a valid way of communicating. Explore language variation and academic language through an inquiry approach, and develop grading policies that do not disadvantage students because of language differences. Culturally responsive instruction values students' cultures and languages and challenges students to use language in ways that enhance their potential.

CHAPTER 9

LANGUAGE TRANSFER

A generous reading of student writing includes noticing the literacy knowledge a student already has in place even when they are learning English as a new language. When we understand something about how literacy knowledge transfers, we see how students are making predictions about how the English language works.

A student's prior knowledge of basic literacy can transfer from one language to another as shown by second grader Arturo's research questions about Bald Eagles (Table 9.1). Arturo had recently moved to the United States from Mexico.

The literacy knowledge Arturo transferred from Spanish to English included using library books for research, writing questions, and word knowledge. He transitioned between Spanish and English, first writing eagle then *las aguilas*. He wrote *juevos* then eggs. Arturo was using his knowledge of concepts and words in Spanish to write in English.

Arturo's teacher spoke only English, so she included the students' families in the projects. The students began thinking of questions in class then took their paper home to discuss them with their families. Later, Arturo brought these questions to the school library and used Spanish and English books to learn about Bald Eagles. His teacher and the school librarian

Student Writing: Give It a Generous Reading, pages 79–85.
Copyright © 2014 by Information Age Publishing
All rights of reproduction in any form reserved.

TABLE 9.1. Arturo's Questions

¿Como se cuidansusjuevos?	*How do they care for their eggs?*
eagle eats the Fish?	
lasaguilas son los aves de presa?	*Are eagles birds of prey?*
lasaguilaforman un grupo?	*Do eagles form a group?*
An eagle lays eggs in trees?	

helped him write about what he learned and the result was his very first English composition.

Inquiry is a powerful and motivating way to build on students' prior knowledge and transfer their literacy knowledge to English writing. Each student in Arturo's class chose a topic they were interested in. Some students chose to learn about a famous person, some chose to learn about an animal. One girl chose to write about *tortillas,* Mexican flat bread. The teacher collaborated with the school librarian to help the children access Spanish and English library books, reference materials, and the Internet (Spence, 2009).

The students in this class spoke varying amounts of English. Arturo was a new immigrant working alongside children who were native English speakers and other children who grew up speaking Spanish at home in the United States. Each of the children developed new literacy skills through pursuing their inquiry project and made use of literacy skills they already possessed.

TYPES OF TRANSFER

English learners who read and write in their home language will transfer this knowledge to reading and writing in English (Cummins, 2001). For example, very young children may know how to choose a book from the library based on the book's cover and illustrations. They may know how to turn the pages and understand the story based on the illustrations. Older students may understand how to read informational texts versus fiction. They may have study skills they can apply. They may understand how to structure their writing, how to use punctuation, and how to use reference materials. This literacy knowledge and more transfers from one language to another.

Latin- and Greek-based languages such as English, Spanish, French, and German have similar alphabets. In these languages, the alphabetic principal that sounds are represented by letters transfers from one language to another. As students learn the new sounds and letters in the target language, they can begin reading and writing (Lindsey, Manis, & Bailey, 2003).

In fact, reading and writing can provide a purpose and context for learning new sounds and letters. Like Arturo, they can begin to read and write even in the beginning stages of language learning.

Of course, there are many instances when linguistic knowledge does not transfer to a new language. There may be differences in word order within a sentence. In Spanish, the adjective usually follows a noun, as in "*el pajaro azul.*" In English, the adjective usually precedes the noun, as in "the blue bird." Letters that look the same are sometimes pronounced differently. In Spanish "ll" is pronounced as a "y" or "j" sound, as in "*¿Como te llama?*" What is your name?

Certain literacy knowledge does not transfer completely. I knew how to write a letter to the parents of school children in English, but I had to learn to be much more formal in writing a letter to parents in Spanish. Many cultures include special phrases and introductory remarks in letter writing that we do not use in the United States. In spite of these differences, there are still many ways that literacy knowledge transfers between languages.

Students transfer literacy knowledge even when their home language does not have an alphabetic script similar to English. For example, bilingual children often learn to write their names in their home language first. Then they transfer the concepts of name and identity to English writing (Kabuto, 2010). Kabuto's research illustrates the sociocultural nature of writing, which entails how one perceives herself in relation to the social situation. Multilingual writers can choose between multiple writing systems according to the context. They can align themselves with one group or another through the writing system they choose.

When students learn a new writing system, they already know that symbols represent language and the symbols are arranged sequentially (Cook & Bassetti, 2005). In addition, students gain a meta-awareness of language as they move between two or more writing systems. They begin to think about how language is structured. They understand there will be patterns and rules unique to each writing system (Kenner, Kress, Al-Khatib, Kam, & Tsai, 2004). Students learning a new writing system understand that print conveys information and is meaningful.

Literacy knowledge is transferred in common, everyday situations. English learners begin to read their environment, including signs, menus, billboards, posters, and other print sources. They begin to write their own names, their friends' names, and words that are important, necessary, or of interest to them. We can build on this capacity to transfer literacy knowledge by bringing student names and environmental print into the classroom. Food labels and other everyday objects with print can be used. For example, a class book can be made with labels from each students' breakfast food attached to a page with a sentence or two such as, "Arturo eats oatmeal for breakfast."

COGNATES AND LOAN WORDS

Cummins (2005) describes how to use the principal of language transfer by teaching students to notice cognates in languages such as Spanish and English, which derive from Latin and Greek (see Table 9.2 for examples). Cognates are words in different languages that have the same derivation. One of Arturo's questions included cognates: "¿Las aguilas forman un grupo?" This was an opportunity to teach him to say and write, "Eagles form groups" using the cognates *forman,* form, *grupos,* and groups.

A writing workshop environment is a great place for teaching with cognates. For example, Arturo was engaged in a research project in which he generated questions then used Spanish and English library books to find the answers. His teacher made time to sit with him as he wrote, guiding him in using the books, making writing decisions, spelling words, and composing sentences. The writing conference is the perfect time to use cognates to expand students' vocabularies in both languages while writing about an interesting topic.

You can introduce cognates to the whole class through a 3-column chart on a large poster. Give a few examples that students might already know, then have the students generate possibilities. Write the English word in the first column. The second column is for the cognate in another language.

TABLE 9.2   Cognates

English	Spanish	German	French	Phillipino
photo	foto	foto	photo	
hotel	hotel	hotel	hôtel	hotel
is	es	ist	est	
fruit	fruta		fruit	
enter	entrar		entrer	
visit	visitar		visiter	bisitahin
guide	guía		guider	
liberty	libertad		liberté	
breeze	brisa	brise	brise	
design	diseño	design		disenyo
relative	relativo	relativen	relatif	
region	región	region	región	rehiyon
acid	acido		acide	asido
plumbing	plomería		plomberie	
chemical	químico	chemisch	chimique	kimiko
biology	biología	biologie	biologie	byolohiya

The third column is for the possibility that students will suggest a false cognate. False cognates are words that sound similar but have completely different meanings. For example, in English, exit means the way out. In Spanish, éxito means a success.

Examples of true cognates are photo (English and French) and *foto* (Spanish and German). Both words mean pictures taken with a camera. Some cognates are spelled the same while others are spelled differently. Some cognates are pronounced and spelled very differently, but still have a recognizable derivation, such as chemical (English) and *químico* (Spanish).

You can also use cognates in reading instruction. Before students read independently, refer to the 3-column chart and remind them to notice cognates, but to be aware of false cognates. Noticing known cognates will enhance their reading comprehension.

Students can also be taught to recognize loan words in other languages. Loan words are words borrowed from another language. Some loan words keep the original spelling, as in "hamburger" (German, English, Bosnian). Other loan words are adapted to mimic the sounds of the new language, as in the Japanese word for hamburger—*hānbāga*. In this pronunciation, the "a" sound is held a bit longer. Japanese includes a growing number of loan words borrowed from English and other languages.

Loan words, like "hamburger," can even cross multiple languages. This is especially common with technical and scientific terms. Examples of technical words are video and computer, shown in Table 9.3. These words are the same or similar in Spanish, Japanese, Korean, and Bosnian.

TABLE 9.3. Loan Words

English	Spanish	Japanese	Korean	Bosnian
fork		fōku	pokeu	
orange		orenji	olenji	
hamburger	hamburguesa	*hānbāga*	haembeogeo	hamburger
cake		kēki	keikeu	
restaurant	restaurante	resutoran		restoran
hotel	hotel	hoteru	hotel	hotel
baseball	béisbol	bēsubēru		bejzbol
skateboard		sukētobēdo	Seukeiteu bodeu	skejtbord
t-shirt		tishātsu	t-syeocheu	
jeans	jeans	jīnzu		
computer	computador	konpyūta	keompyuteo	kompjuter
video	vídeo	bideo	bidio	video

We commonly use brand names and pop culture terms from other languages. Japanese words such as *Honda*, a well-known auto manufacturer, and *anime*, a comic book art form, have entered the English language. Some other loan words appear in Table 9.3. Notice that these words include popular foods, clothing, sports, and technology—all common sources for loan words.

We think of English as one language, yet it is influenced by many languages. Some English words derive from languages such as Latin or German. These words might be both loan words and cognates. For example, we borrowed "hamburger" from German, and *hamburguesa* is a Spanish cognate.

Students can have a lot of fun with language. If you are lucky enough to have a mixture of many languages spoken in your classroom, use them as a resource for learning. Students who speak another language have an expertise that can be drawn upon to engage the whole class in language study. I have included some ideas for using language transfer in this chapter, but the possibilities are limitless and will differ based on the students in your own classroom.

Remember that many literacy concepts transfer across languages. Students can begin to read and write while they are beginning to learn new sounds and letters in English. They can use what they know about books, writing, and studying because this knowledge transfers across languages. Draw upon your students' linguistic knowledge and encourage them to continue developing their home language so they will become multilingual and multiliterate.

IDEAS FOR INSTRUCTION

- Language partners—A native English speaker is paired with a speaker of another language. They teach each other how to correctly pronounce the cognates in each other's language. They practice the word until they can say it fluently.
- Word detectives—Word walls of cognates are created by students when they become word detectives, finding and collecting words from their homes, dictionaries, language teachers, and other adults who speak different languages.
- Stop and think—Mini-lessons are taught right before independent reading. The teacher demonstrates how to stop and think about possible cognates while reading a passage aloud. Then the students are reminded to notice cognates in their personal, independent reading.
- Sounds like—A reading passage is projected onto a screen for the whole class to see and read. Then a word with a cognate in the stu-

dents' home language is highlighted. The class is asked to think of words in their languages that sound like the highlighted word.
- Word list interviews—After completing class activities with cognates, students are given a list of words that have cognates in other languages. They interview their parents, other family members, caretakers, or friends to learn cognates for the words.
- 3-column chart—The first column is for the English word. The second column is for the cognate in another language. The third column is for the possibility students will come up with a false cognate. Begin with cognates you know your students will be familiar with, then have them add their own ideas to the chart.
- Cognates in reading—Encourage students to notice cognates in their independent reading. Make sure they are aware of the possibility of false cognates.
- Writing conferences—Sit down next to a student to help with in-progress writing. Help the student make decisions about her writing, such as which language to use, how to paraphrase information from a source, how to spell tricky words, and to introduce new vocabulary she may need for her writing.
- Bilingual books—Books written in your students' home language and English have many uses. Read these books for enjoyment. Encourage students to take the books home to share with their families. Use informational bilingual books for inquiry and research projects.
- Alphabet books—Make a book with each letter of the English alphabet. Draw or attach magazine pictures of items that begin with the letter in either English or the home language.
- Class books of labels—Each student brings a label from a food product from home. It is attached to a page and the student writes a sentence or two under the label.
- Family & friends' names—Provide students with text frames for writing about friends and family. They fill in the blanks with names and information. My name is ____. I have ____ brothers. Their names are ____, ____, and ____.

CHAPTER 10

LITERARY DEVICES

This chapter includes an annotated glossary of literary devices intended as a resource for reference and learning. It includes different figures of speech, as well as other devices such as irony. It also contains literary elements such as mood and theme.

Generous reading involves *finding* literary devices and elements in writing. It is not intended for adding literary devices. Since these devices are part of everyday speech, students may write with them without being consciously aware of them.

On the other hand, some pieces of writing will not contain figures of speech because they are not a part of the student's way of speaking or because the genre of writing does not lend itself to figurative language. However, when literary devices are noticed by teachers, a new depth of understanding occurs and instructional conversations are enhanced. Literary elements are also included in this glossary and are helpful for understanding student writing. This resource can help you as you begin generous reading of student writing.

Each literary device is defined and includes an example from student writing. A brief explanation of how the example relates to the definition is included. This section concludes with ideas for using this information for planning instruction.

FIGURES OF SPEECH

Hyperbole	Exaggeration for effect. *They were having a lifetime of fun.* The amount of fun is compared to the amount that could be experienced in a lifetime.
Metaphor	An implied comparison of two different things or ideas. *We are facing battle with cancer, heart disease, and other sickness. But the worst is a big dog. Drugs and alcohol.* A battle is compared to solving problems and a big dog is compared to a having a problem.
Simile	An expressed comparison of two different things or ideas. *Eating this sandwich is like biting into a slice of heaven.* The sandwich is directly compared to a slice of heaven using the word like.
Symbol	A literal construct that stands for an abstract concept. *When we came back my fish was dead. That was almost the happiest memory ever.* The dead fish stands for the happy memory that was ruined.
Synecdoche	Expressions where a part is substituted for the whole or the whole for a part. *It keeps young people off the streets.* The streets stand for dangerous urban areas.

OTHER LITERARY DEVICES

Alliteration	The repetition of the same first sound in a group of words. *Silver started to stare at me.* "S" and "st" are repeated.
Allusion	Mentioning a famous text to reference complex ideas. *Anne Frank was killed because she was Jewish.* *The Diary of Anne Frank* references the Holocaust.
Antithesis	Opposite pairs of words or phrases. *It's good for rainy days and sunny days.* Rainy and sunny are opposites.

Flashback	Interrupting the narrative to present previous events.
	Something bad happened, but here's how it all happened.
	The narrator first wrote as a 9-year-old then began writing about an event that happened when he was younger.
Foreshadowing	Words or phrases that hint at what will happen later in a story, without giving away the plot.
	One sunny day, mom and I were moving into a new house. The house looked kind of old, but I didn't care.
	The narrator briefly notes the condition of the house. She later finds out the house is haunted.
Imagery	Words or images that help the reader visualize.
	The little turtle was caught.
	The word "little" creates an image of a helpless animal.
Irony	Suggesting that something is not as it seems to be.
	She went back to sleep and everything was all right. Or was it?
	Previous events in the story suggested that something terrible could again happen to this character who believes that everything is all right.
Onomatopoeia	Words that sound like the thing they refer to.
	The door opened—creak.
	"Creak" is the sound of a rusty door hinge.
Oxymoron	The combination of contradictory terms that explores a deeper meaning.
	I looked in and saw an ugly doll.
	One expects a doll to be pretty or cute, so this combination has an unnerving effect.
Personification	Human traits given to nonhuman things.
	The playground that I have in my mind was joyful.
	The playground is given the human trait of joy.
Repetition	Using a word or phrase two or more times for effect.
	We do it step by step by step.
	"Step by step" is repeated.
Rhyme	The repetition of the ending sound in a group of words.
	The lights in the night.
	The sound "ight" is repeated.

LITERARY ELEMENTS

Characterization
: Introducing and developing aspects of a character.

    Hank and Roger rushed to the tree to stop Rascal, but it was too late. Rascal was already at the top of the tree. "What are you doing?" said Hank and Roger worriedly. "I'll be okay, don't worry about me," said Rascal, frightened.

    The action, dialogue, and the adverbs, "worried" and "frightened" reveal character traits.

Conflict
: Discord between characters, between a character and the environment, or within a character.

    It's so fun to dance, even though sometimes it is really hard to understand how someone is dancing, but we have to do it.

    An example of conflict within the character, who enjoys dancing, but repeatedly states the difficulties involved and the need for perseverance.

Mood
: Words and phrases used to portray feeling.

    It looked abandoned and scary, but they still went in.

    A feeling of unease and that something bad will happen is portrayed.

Plot
: The story's sequence of events.

    On a cool summer night . . . Then out of nowhere . . . Then Romeo went home.

    These are some key phrases that indicate the sequence of events.

Point of View
: The perception from which a story is told.

    She saw a frog. She asked, "Where am I at, Mrs. Frog?"

    This story is told in third person using personal pronouns, proper nouns, and dialogue.

Setting
: Establishment of the time, place, and mood of a story

    On a Saturday night at 11:40 p.m., a stranger walked across the neighborhood.

    The time is 11:40 p.m., the place is the neighborhood, the mood is implied by late night and introducing a stranger into the setting. Stating the exact time is typical of detective stories.

Tension	A point in a story that contributes to a strained or suspenseful quality.
	She came closer and closer.
	This builds the feeling that something significant is about to happen.
Theme	An implied or expressed idea presented throughout the text.
	It was my best day ever.
	The author listed many delightful things that happened throughout the day and summed up the theme with this sentence.

Notice that you will sometimes find combinations of literary devices. The phrase "it's good for rainy days and sunny days" contains antithesis in "rainy" and "sunny." It also contains repetition of the word "days." Literary devices can also do double duty in a composition. The repetition of "she came closer and closer" grabs your attention, but it also develops tension in the story.

The examples in this glossary all came from 3rd- and 5th-grade writing. The genres of writing were fiction, persuasive essay, expository, personal narrative, and fantasy. Finding literary devices in fiction, fantasy, and personal narrative is common. Finding them in persuasive essay and expository writing is a little less common, but also useful. It reveals some of the ways students are using language to construct meaningful prose. Literary devices are essential for writing one of the most popular types of text: narrative nonfiction. Narrative nonfiction can be found in popular books and magazines on topics such as health, finance, food, and sports. Literacy devices are important to almost all types of writing.

This glossary is not meant as a list of topics to teach students. For very young students, words such as "antithesis" may just be confusing and not have much educative value. On the other hand, teachers of young children will use vocabulary such as "rhyme" and "setting."

For upper elementary through middle school students, literary devices can and should be used in order to expose students to this vocabulary. However, words such as "antithesis" are not appropriate for rote memorization at this age. Simile, metaphor, flashback, plot, and tension are appropriate words to use during class discussions and individual writing conferences. Depending on the age of the students, use the literary terms, but don't expect them to memorize these words or their definitions. Just let the students know they are writing in ways that are common in literature.

USING LITERARY DEVICES FOR INSTRUCTION

The best writing instruction happens in a writing workshop environment. This type of classroom environment encourages student choice of topic, talk between students, and sharing of written work. The teacher acts as facilitator and more experienced writer. Genre study, writer's notebooks, and projects make up the curriculum.

This is in contrast to a curriculum made up of prompts such as, "What is your favorite place? Describe that place using the five senses." Prompts are not conducive to creativity and expression because students may not have experiences that connect with the prompt. Or the prompt may not inspire them to write more than a cursory answer. Prompts are limiting; writing workshop is expansive.

The structure of writing workshop includes the following:

- A minilesson in which the teacher demonstrates some aspect of writing
- An extended amount of time for individual writing
- Individual writing conferences between students and between teacher and students
- Sharing finished writing with the whole class or other audiences.

Many excellent books have been written on how to teach writing within a writing workshop. I highly recommend these: *The Art of Teaching Writing* (Calkins, 1986), *The Writer's Notebook* (Fletcher, 1996), *Writer's Workshop* (Ray & Laminack, 2001), *Hidden Gems* (Bomer, 2010), *From Ideas to Words* (Laman, 2013), and *Writing Instruction for English Learners* (Mora-Flores, 2009). Rather than reiterate what these excellent authors do so well, I will focus on how to use your knowledge of literary devices for instruction within the writing workshop structure.

MINILESSONS

The minilesson, as the name implies is short—about 10 to 15 minutes. Once you have used generous reading to discover literary devices in one piece of writing, you can use this knowledge to teach a minilesson. You may find that many of your students could benefit from such a lesson. For example, a fifth grader, Trey, wrote an essay about the problems of drugs and alcohol in society. You notice he used two metaphors: "We are facing battle with cancer, heart disease and other sickness. But the worst is a big dog. Drugs and alcohol."

This can be used to teach a number of things, but the first thing I would do is ask the students' permission to share the essay, then perhaps he would read it aloud to the class while projecting it onto a screen. I would admire his use metaphors and ask the class what they thought "big dog" meant in this context. Since metaphors such as this are fairly common in the southern United States, where this student lives, I would ask if other students could contribute figures of speech they might know of. This is a culturally responsive lesson that acknowledges the unique language of the area.

Minilessons are best when they address the writing needs of the class as a whole. If I notice that punctuation instruction would benefit many students, I plan a punctuation lesson. I would teach how to transform Trey's sentences by using different types of punctuation. Trey chose to use periods to create three separate sentences. He could also have used a comma or dash between the last two sentences. I would point out that "Drugs and alcohol" is not a complete sentence, but I would also acknowledge that sometimes authors use incomplete sentences for a special effect, referring to a youth or children's book to illustrate this point. This type of lesson contextualizes grammar, making the concept easier to understand and apply.

When teaching grammar in context, I develop an anchor chart to hang on the classroom wall. For a focus on writing complete sentences, I would write "Sentences" at the top and elicit generalizations from the class, such as "has a noun or pronoun and a verb." This chart can be added to over time and serves as an anchor to come back to in future conversations about sentence grammar.

Metaphor is an appropriate concept to teach in fifth grade, so this is another possible minilesson. For this lesson, I would use the discovery method. I would ask Trey to read his essay while projecting it onto a screen. I would ask the students to find unusual figures of speech and see what they find on their own. Once they have found a metaphor, I would define metaphor and ask them to find another one in the essay. In the three sentences above, there are two: "We are facing a battle" and "The worst is a big dog." Teaching metaphor within the context of student writing helps make the concept familiar and usable.

WRITING CONFERENCES

Writing conferences are used to meet the needs of individuals and to give students the opportunity to talk about their writing. During a writing workshop, the teacher meets either with students who have requested a conference or those the teacher identified as needing attention. Students can also meet with one another to read drafts of writing in order to get feedback from their peers. Teacher and students confer while the other students are writing, researching, or illustrating.

There are several ways generous reading can be used during writing conferences. Just as Trey's writing was used in a whole-class minilesson, similar lessons can be given on an individual basis if the topic is not relevant to the whole class. Another way to use generous reading in a conference is to talk through the generous reading form for students (see Appendix).

First, help the student find voices in the writing. Then help the student find literary devices in the writing. Jot down notes on the form regarding what this tells you about the writer and how the writer can use this knowledge to improve the piece he or she is working on.

Once you have used the generous reading form for students during writing conferences, your students may be able to use the form with their classmates during peer conferences. You will be able to judge whether your students understand the concepts enough to use generous reading on their own. You may want to adapt the form to include a list of literary devices that are age appropriate. For 3rd-grade students, the list may include simile, imagery, characterization, and setting. Literary devices are abstract language concepts that take a degree of sophistication to understand, yet students often surprise us by rising to such challenging tasks.

Finding the literary devices and voices in student writing allows us to see the complex ways students are using language. It takes us beyond the requirements of rubrics and grade-level standards and opens a window into the world of the writer.

APPENDIX

1. Generous Reading Form
2. GR Open Form
3. GR Student Form for Students
4. Ideas for Teaching English Learners
5. Aspects of the Person, Writer, and Writing
6. Generous Reading Chanxuan

STUDENT WRITING: GIVE IT A GENEROUS READING

GENEROUS READING FORM

Student   Date   Grade   Teacher

Genre   Process Stage   Title

Voices of Others	**Figurative or Descriptive Language**
What are the voices in this piece?	What figurative or descriptive language is in this piece?

What does this tell you about the person?

What does this tell you about the writer?

What does this reveal about the piece?

What is the student doing especially well that I want to reinforce?

What can I teach that will help the student grow as a person or as a writer?

What can I teach that will help improve this piece or future writing?

Student notes: English learner (level), AAE Dialect, Gender.

GENEROUS READING OPEN FORM

What are the voices in this piece?	What figurative or descriptive language is in this piece?

What does this tell you about the person?

What does this tell you about the writer?

What does this reveal about the piece?

What is the student doing especially well that I want to reinforce? What can I teach that will help the student grow as a person or as a writer? What can I teach that will help improve this piece or future writing?

GENEROUS READING OPEN FORM FOR STUDENTS

Name	Date
Title	

Voices	Descriptive Language

What does this tell you about the writing?	

How can you improve this piece?	

IDEAS FOR TEACHING ENGLISH LEARNERS

Beginning

- Students will learn to communicate with their classmates by being involved in the classroom.
- They will go through a silent period when they do not speak much, but are soaking in the sound of English.
- Teach English letters, sounds, words, and grammar in context and multiple exposures with songs, chants, poems, and games.
- Language learning is communication

Speaking in the classroom

- Learn some of the student's language.
- Greeting the student in their home language and learning a few phrases shows you value the language.
- Expect the student to use English for common phrases such as requests and replies (after the silent period).
- Slow down your speech when explaining.
- Repeat important information.
- Begin with "yes" and "no" questions.
- Encourage risk-taking by accepting approximations.
- Involve English learners in all content areas along with the rest of the class.

Communicating
- Encourage communication in all ways possible.
  - Listening, speaking, reading, and writing in home language.
  - Listening, speaking, reading, and writing in English.
- Use computers, educational games, drawing, drama, music.
- Have students draw pictures, write in their home language, or use their emergent English writing to communicate their experiences.
  - Rewrite this information as pages in a book and bind together. These books can be used for beginning English reading texts.
  - Parents can help with this project by helping to make the books bilingual. These books can be read at home.
- Use language experience stories.

(continues)

ASPECTS OF THE PERSON, WRITER, AND WRITING

This table lists aspects of the person, the writer, and the writing itself, which I found in third graders' writing during the development of generous reading.

Voices

The Person	The Writer	The Writing Itself
Concern for topic	Expresses abstract concepts	Three-point argument
Empathy	Cites historical figures	Introduces topic
Responsibility	Importance of topic	Summarize to conclude
Opinion	Voice of expert	Repetition to reinforce
Critical	Appropriated discourse	Details support
Future	Persuasive language	Knowledge of topic
Concern/Fear	Language of teacher/	Conclusion
Parental authority	classroom	Paragraph-topic sentences
Connects to own life	Internalized content language	Page-topic sentences
Interest	Opinions	Mixed genres
Sustains interest	Informs	Playing with language
Family	Developing English	Explains
Notices world	Emotion	Author's voice
Physical	Dialogue	Appeal to reader
Self-image	Humor	Sentence combining
Enjoyment	Aware of audience	General to specific
Connects concepts	Uses several sign systems	Point of view
Cites authority	Uses Spanish	Genre within genre
Values		Setting
		Mood
		Theme
		Organization
		Conflict
		Action
		Cites sources

Figurative and Descriptive Language

The Person	The Writer	The Writing
Relates topic to life	American popular language	Imagery
Empathy	Bilingual	Author's voice
Concern/Fear	Teacher/classroom language	Historical figures
Misconceptions	Opinions	Supports argument
Concept Connections	Personal experience	Reliance on teacher
Questions world	Responsibility	Cause and effect
Morality	Curiosity	Details
Family importance	Explains	Appeal to audience
Self-image	Persuasive	Concept connections
Values	Examples	Repetition
Physical	Developing English	Voice
Responsibility	Reads world	Mood
Personal Knowledge	Several sign systems	Moral
Imagination	Observations	Introduction
Connects with people		Persuasive
Respects authority		Plays with language
		Genre within genre

Figurative and Descriptive Language		
The Person	**The Writer**	**The Writing**
		Theme
		Setting
		High point
		Subplot
		Action
		Organization
		Time
		Spanish
		Symbol
		Cites sources
		Used content language

GENEROUS READING

Date	Grade: 7	Student: Chanxuan	Teacher: Xumai
Genre: personal narrative	Process stage: final Title: My first time to the U.S.—My first day at school		
Voices of Others		Figurative/Descriptive Language	
What are the voices in this piece?		What figurative/descriptive language is in this	
"Oh, my gosh!" – kids' talk It really took me a long while- friends & their parents who had travelled to the U.S. My teacher is very thoughtful- Chanxuan's mom I even made a new friend- kids' talk if you treat everybody friendly, you will get friendly treatment as well – Chinese saying		Time is like a drop of water. It just infuses into the ocean. The school in my mind was like a big open, bloody mouth of a bear. It may swallow me into its stomach any time. Even to me, this "foreigner" I even made a new friend Step by step, marching to school	

What does this tell you about the person?
She is creative and uses her reading to create something new in her own writing.

What does this tell you about the writer?
She can use metaphors effectively.
It shows her passion.
She uses her reading to create her writing.

What does this reveal about the writing?
It is passionate and detailed. It has strong voice, even the punctuation makes the voice strong.
It has a complete structure including an introduction, several events, and an ending.
It follows chronological order.

What is the student doing especially well that I want to reinforce?
She uses the metaphors, drops of water for time and the bear for school. Her use of small words such as "even" help convey the mood.

What can I teach that will help the student grow as a person or as a writer?
Extend a short writing to a long writing by including places and cultural details. A writer should know a lot.

What can I teach that will help improve this piece or future writing?
Show her how adding specific foods and places she talked about with her new friend would expand the writing. Show her in her books, such as the "Warrior" series that the author uses specific geographical and other details.

Student notes: female, fluent Mandarin Chinese speaker
English is at a conversational level

REFERENCES

AACAP. (2011). *Children and TV violence. Facts for families.* Retrieved September 18, 2013, from http://www.aacap.org/App_Themes/AACAP/docs/facts_for_families/13_children_and_tv_violence.pdf
Anderson, C. (2000). *How's it going?* Portsmouth, NH: Heinemann.
Armstrong, M. (2006). *Children writing stories.* Berkshire, UK: Open University Press.
Bakhtin, M. (1981). *Discourse in the novel.* Austin: University of Texas Press.
Bakhtin, M. (1986). *Speech genres & other late essays.* Austin: University of Texas Press.
Bear, D. R., Invernizzi, M., Templeton, S., & Johnson, F. (2012). *Words their way: Word study for phonics, vocabulary, and spelling instruction* (5th ed.). Upper Saddle River, NJ: Pearson.
Bomer, K. (2010). *Hidden gems.* Portsmouth, NH: Heinemann.
Breuch, L. M. K. (2002). Post-process "pedagogy": A philosophical exercise. In V. Villanueva (Ed.), *Cross-talk in comp theory: A reader* (2nd ed., pp. 97–125). Urbana, IL: NCTE.
Calkins, L. M. (1986). *The art of teaching writing.* Portsmouth, NH: Heinemann.
Canagarajah, A. S. (2006a). TESOL at forty: What are the issues? *TESOL Quarterly, 40,* 9–34.
Canagarajah, A. S. (2006b). Toward a writing pedagogy of shuttling between languages: Learning from multilingual writers. *College English, 68,* 589–604.
Charity Hudley, A. R., & Mallinson, C. (2011). *Understanding English language variation in U.S. schools.* New York, NY: Teachers College Press.

Cook, V. J., & Bassetti, B. (Eds.). (2005). *Second language writing systems*. Clevedon, UK: Multilingual Matters.

Cummins, J. (2001). *Negotiating identities: Education for empowerment in a diverse society* (2nd ed.). Los Angeles: California Association for Bilingual Education.

Cummins, J. (2005) A proposal for action: Strategies for recognizing heritage language competence as a learning resource within the mainstream classroom. *The Modern Language Journal, 89,* 585–592.

Donohue, T. (2008). Cross-cultural analysis of student writing: Beyond discourses of difference. *Written Communication, 25*(3), 319–352.

Dyson, A. H. (2003). *The brothers and sisters learn to write*. New York, NY: Teachers College Press.

Dyson, A. H., & Smitherman, G. (2009). The right (write) start: African American language and the discourse of sounding right. *Teacher's College Record, 111,* 973–998.

Fletcher, R. (1996). *A writer's notebook: Unlocking the writer within you*. New York, NY: Avon.

Graves, D. (1983). *Writing: Teachers and children at work*. Portsmouth, NH: Heinemann.

Greenfield, E. (2003). *Honey I love, and other love poems*. New York, NY: Harper Collins.

Halasek, K. (1999). *A pedagogy of possibility: Bakhtinian perspectives on composition studies*. Carbondale: Southern Illinois University Press.

Harris, J. (1997). *A teaching subject: Composition since 1966*. Upper Saddle River, NJ: Prentice Hall.

Heard, M. (2008). What should we do with postprocess theory? *Pedagogy, 8,* 283–304.

Jiménez, R. T. (1997). The strategic reading abilities and potential of five low-literacy Latina/o readers in middle school. *Reading Research Quarterly, 32*(3), 224–243.

Kabuto, B. (2010). Bilingual writing as an act of identity: Sign making in multiple scripts. *Bilingual Research Journal, 33,* 130–149.

Kachru, Y., & Smith, L. E. (2008). *Cultures, contexts, and world Englishes*. New York, NY: Routledge.

Karen People. (2010). *Culture, faith and history* [Brochure]. Bendigo, Australia: Karen Buddhist Dhamma Dhutta Foundation.

Kenner, C., Kress, G., Al-Khatib, H., Kam, R., & Tsai, K. (2004). Finding the keys to biliteracy: How young children interpret different writing systems. *Language and Education, 18,* 124–144.

Kent, T. (Ed.). (1999). *Post-process theory: Beyond the writing-process paradigm*. Carbondale: Southern Illinois University Press.

Krashen, S. D. (1987). *Principles and practice in second language acquisition*. New York, NY: Prentice-Hall International.

Krashen, S. D. (1988). *Second language acquisition and second language learning*. New York, NY: Prentice-Hall International.

Kubota, R. (2004). Toward critical contrastive rhetoric. *Journal of Second Language Writing, 13,* 7–27.

Ladson-Billings, G. (1995). Toward a theory of culturally relevant pedagogy. *American Educational Research Journal, 32,* 465–491.

Ladson-Billings, G., & Tate, W. (1995). Toward a critical race theory of education. *Teachers College Record, 97*, 47–68.

Lakoff, G., & Johnson, M. (1980). *Metaphors we live by*. Chicago, IL: Chicago University Press.

Laman, T. T. (2013). *From ideas to words: Writing strategies for English language learners*. Portsmouth, NH: Heinemann.

Lévi-Strauss, C. (1955). The structural study of myth. *The Journal of American Folklore, 68*, 428–444.

Lindsey, K. A., Manis, F. R., & Bailey, C. E. (2003). Prediction of first-grade reading in Spanish-speaking English-language learners. *Journal of Educational Psychology, 95*(3), 482–494.

Malik, A. A. (1990). A psycholinguistic analysis of the reading behavior of EFL proficient readers using culturally familiar and culturally unfamiliar expository texts. *American Educational Research Journal, 27*, 205–223.

Moll, L. C., Amanti, C., Neff, D., & Gonzalez, N. (1992). Funds of knowledge for teaching: Using a qualitative approach to connect homes and classrooms. *Theory Into Practice, 31*, 132–141.

Mora-Flores, E. (2009). *Writing instruction for English learners: A focus on genre*. Thousand Oaks, CA: Corwin.

Murray, D. (1968). *A writer teaches writing: A practical method of teaching composition*. Boston, MA: Houghton Mifflin.

National Commission on Writing. (2003). *The neglected "R"*. New York, NY: College Entrance Examination Board.

National Council of Teachers of Mathematics. (2006). *Principles and standards for school mathematics*. Reston, VA: NCTM.

Nia, I. (1999). Units of study in the writing workshop. *Primary Voices, 8*, 3–9.

Nieto, S. (2002). *Language, culture, and teaching: Critical perspectives for a new century*. Mahwah, NJ: Lawrence Erlbaum.

Piestrup, A. M. (1973). *Black dialect interference and accommodation of reading instruction in first grade*. Monographs of the Language Behavior Research Laboratory, No. 4. Berkeley: University of California.

Ray, K. W., & Laminack, L. (2001). *Writing workshop: Working through the hard parts (and they're all hard parts)*. Urbana, IL: National Council of Teachers of English.

Russek, B. (1998) Writing to learn mathematics. *Plymouth State College Journal on Writing Across the Curriculum, 9*, 36–45.

Shanahan, T., & Shanahan, C. (2008). Teaching disciplinary literacy to adolescents: Rethinking content-area literacy. *Harvard Educational Review, 78*, 40–59.

Spence, L. K. (2008). Generous reading: Discovering dialogic voices in writing. *English in Education, 4*, 253–268.

Spence, L. K. (2009). Inquiry based writing workshop. *Teacher Librarian, 37*, 23–27.

Spence, L. K. (2010a). Discerning writing assessment: Insights into an analytical rubric. *Language Arts, 87*, 337–347.

Spence, L. K. (2010b). Generous reading: Seeing students through their writing. *The Reading Teacher, 63*, 634–642.

Spence, L. K., & Cardenas-Cortez, K. (2011). Writing gave me a voice: A Spanish-dominant teacher's writing workshop. *TESOL Journal, 18*, 1–23.

TESOL International Association. (2006). *Standards.* Retrieved September, 18, 2013, from http://www.tesol.org/advance-the-field/standards

Tobin, J. (2000). *"Good guys don't wear hats": Children's talk about the media.* New York, NY: Teachers College Press.

Valdés, G., & Figueroa, R. A. (1994). *Bilingualism and testing: A special case of bias.* Norwood, NJ: Ablex.

VanSledright, B. (2002). Confronting history's interpretive paradox while teaching fifth graders to investigate the past. *American Educational Research Journal, 39,* 1089–1115.

Voloshinov, V. (1976). Discourse in life and discourse in art. In N. Bruss (Ed.), *Freudianism: A Marxist critique* (I. R. Titunik, Trans.). New York, NY: Academic.

Vygotsky, L. (1986). *Thought and language.* Cambridge, MA: MIT Press.

Weaver, C. (2008). *Grammar to enrich and enhance writing.* NJ: Heinemann.

Yore, L. D., Hand, B., Goldman, S. R., Hildebrand, G. M., Osborne, J. F., Treagust, D. F., & Wallace, C. S. (2004). New directions in language and science education research. *Reading Research Quarterly, 39,* 347–352.

AUTHOR BIOGRAPHY

Lucy K. Spence is an associate professor of Language and Literacy at the University of South Carolina. Spence received her Ph.D. in Curriculum and Instruction from Arizona State University in 2006.

Seventeen years teaching children in a predominately Spanish-speaking community formed the foundation for her research on linguistically diverse student writing. She has developed Generous Reading, a method of looking closely at student writing in order to notice the strengths and unique aspects of student writing. Teachers use this formative assessment to design instruction for individual students. She has published articles on this work in English in Education and The Reading Teacher.

Her research on English learners has been published in TESOL Journal, The Bilingual Research Journal, and other peer-reviewed journals. She teaches literacy courses at the undergraduate and graduate level in the Department of Instruction and Teacher Education at the University of South Carolina.

SUBJECT INDEX

AACAP, 64, 103
Academic
  language, 74, 75, 77
  vocabulary, 22, 29, 33, 38, 75
Adjectives, 28
Affective filter, 73
African American English, 8, 13, 46, 47, 49, 50, 73,
Alliteration, 15, 26, 27, 28, 34, 88
Anderson, 51, 103
Answerability, 4, 6, 7, 9, 17
Armstrong, ix, 4, 103
Assessment, 3, 5, 13, 22, 31, 32, 33, 48, 56, 64, 65, 76, 105, 107

Bakhtin, ix, 4, 6, 103, 104
Bilingual, ix, 26, 41, 44, 71, 73, 81, 85, 99, 100, 104, 106, 107
Bomer, ix, 92, 103
Breuch, viii, 103

Calkins, viii, 17, 92, 103
Canagarajah, 45, 47, 103

Character, 13, 25, 43, 47, 51, 64, 71, 89, 90, 94
Charity Hudley, 46, 73, 103
Chinese, viii, ix, 41, 42, 43, 44, 47, 102
Close reading, 4
Cognates, 82, 83, 84, 85
  false, 83, 85
Communicative flexibility, 48, 49
Concepts
  Bakhtin's, 6,
  development, 2, 30, 39, 40, 52, 55, 56, 59, 60, 64, 75, 79, 100
  generous reading, 2, 94
  transfer, 81, 84
Constructivist, 75
Content,
  subject area, 41, 57, 58, 59, 60, 61, 73, 75, 76, 99, 100, 101, 105
  writing, 3, 45, 76
Conventions, 2, 3, 30
Cook, 81, 104
Correction method, 49

Critical, ix, 4, 9, 40, 68, 72, 100, 104, 105,
Cultural motifs, 72, 77
Culturally relevant, x, 72, 104
Culture
  ethnic, 15, 17, 24, 25, 38, 40, 45, 48, 51, 52, 72, 77, 81, 104
  in curriculum, 52, 72, 75, 77, 105
  in student writing, x, 5, 28, 33, 46, 47, 57, 104
  popular, 5, 13, 17, 24, 25, 84
  school, 25
Cummins, 80, 82, 104

Demonstration, 21, 36, 41
Descriptive language, 16, 19, 22, 33, 42, 58, 68, 96, 97, 98, 100, 101, 102
Details, 17, 18, 19, 28, 60, 67, 100, 102
Dialogue, viii, 6, 7, 8, 9, 25, 63, 90, 100
Dictionaries, 27, 38, 40, 47, 84
Donohue, 4, 104
Dyson, viii, 48, 104

English
  academic, 74, 75
  acquisition/proficiency levels, 13, 33
  African American, viii, 8, 13, 46, 47, 49, 50, 73
  learners, viii, 2, 3, 8, 11, 18, 22, 30, 31, 32, 33, 40, 44, 64, 66, 69, 73, 75, 76, 80, 81, 92, 95, 96, 99, 105, 107
  phonics, 31, 103
  Southern American, viii, 26, 46, 47, 74, 93
  standardized, 9, 26, 31, 32, 46, 49, 74
  vocabulary, 15, 39
  world, ix, x, 8, 46, 47, 48, 104

Feedback, 2, 3, 7, 19, 73, 93
Figurative, 27, 28, 42, 96, 100, 101, 102
Figures of speech, 88
Fletcher, 92, 104

Generous reading
  form, viii, ix, x, 12, 13, 15, 16, 19, 21, 43, 64, 93, 94, 95, 96
  method, 9, 11

Genre, 11, 12, 13, 51, 87, 91, 92, 96, 100, 102, 103, 105
Grading, 19, 76, 77
Grammar, 17, 19, 22, 26, 33, 40, 41, 47, 64, 75, 76, 77, 93, 99, 106
Graves, viii, 17, 104

Halasek, 17, 104
Heard, viii, 104
Heritage language, 41, 73, 104
Home language, ix, 13, 15, 17, 28, 31, 33, 39, 40, 41, 44, 52, 73, 80, 81, 84, 85, 99
History writing, x, 55, 58, 59, 60, 106
Hybrid language, 4, 5, 6
Hyperbole, 28, 66, 88

Identity, ix, 59, 65, 72, 77, 81, 104
Imagery, 18, 89, 94, 100
Immersion, 41, 59

Jiménez, 51, 104
Journals, 60, 74, 76

Kabuto, 81, 104
Karen, viii, ix, 35, 36, 37, 38, 39, 40, 104
Kenner, 81, 104
Kent, viii, 104
Krashen, 73, 104

Ladson-Billings, 51, 72, 104, 105
Lakoff, ix, 105
Laman, 92, 105
Learning, x, 22, 27, 28
Lévi-Strauss, ix, 105
Lindsey, 80, 105
Linguistic diversity, viii, x, 22, 31, 32
Literary
  analysis, 9, 64, 65
  devices, 28, 33, 87, 88, 91, 92, 94
  elements, x, 15, 16, 17, 18, 19, 26, 27, 28, 34, 40, 56, 66, 68, 87, 90
Loan words, 82, 83, 84

Malik, 51, 105
Math writing, x, 13, 55, 56, 57, 58, 60, 105
Media, 9, 13, 24, 25, 33, 47, 48, 106
Metacognitive, 49, 51, 53

Metaphor, vii, ix, 15, 17, 27, 28, 41, 42, 88, 91, 92, 93, 102, 105
Mexican, 15, 17, 18, 24, 51, 80
Minilessons, 30, 50, 53, 67, 84, 92, 93
Moll, 52, 105
Mood, 1, 17, 18, 28, 51, 87, 90, 100, 102
Mora-Flores, 91, 105
Multicultural
  curriculum, 48, 52
  literature, 50, 51, 52
Multimodal, 60
Murray, viii, 17, 105

National Commission on Writing, 60, 105
National Council of Teachers of Mathematics, 55, 105
Narrative, ix, 1, 6, 13, 22, 23, 26, 27, 28, 29, 30, 31, 32, 42, 43, 44, 71, 72, 89, 91, 102
Nia, 51, 105
Nieto, 48, 72, 105

Onomatopoeia, 15, 63, 64, 89
Organization, 3, 17, 18, 100, 101

Piestrup, 49, 74, 105
Plot, 41, 51, 89, 90, 91, 101
Popular culture, 5, 13, 17, 24, 25, 84
Prepositions, 75
Process, 58, 59, 60
  English learning, 8, 9, 31
  generous reading, 19
  historian, 58
Postprocess, viii, ix, 103, 104
  writing, vii, viii, x, 2, 3, 5, 13, 17, 40, 44, 56, 65, 66, 68, 96, 102, 104
Punctuation, 13, 40, 43, 72, 80, 93, 102

Ray, 92, 105
Reread, 13, 17, 18, 19, 27, 47, 64
Read aloud, 32, 51
Repetition, 26, 28, 33, 34, 50, 57, 88, 89, 91, 100
Response, 1, 2, 5, 6, 7, 8, 9, 32, 33, 43
Rhyme, 15, 26, 28, 89, 91
Rubric, 2, 3, 7, 32, 64, 94, 105
Russek, 56, 105

Science writing, x, 5, 13, 41, 55, 57, 58, 60, 106
Scores, 2, 3, 7, 32
Shanahan, 55, 105
Sharing, 61, 66, 68, 92
Sentence
  African American English, 46, 50
  complex, 58
  fluency, 3, 32
  English construction, 17, 19, 64, 75, 76, 81, 82, 85, 91, 93, 100
  proficiency level, 33
  variation, 67
  Spanish, 39, 81
Simile, 28, 42, 88, 91, 94
Social Studies writing, 35, 41, 59, 60
Sociocultural, viii, 9, 64, 81
Southern American English, viii, 26, 46, 47, 74, 93
Spanish
  cognates, 82, 83, 84
  in English writing, 26, 27, 30, 31, 100, 101
  speakers, viii, ix, 8, 22, 24, 39, 45, 65, 71, 79, 80, 105
Spelling, 1, 3, 22, 31, 33, 38, 40, 47, 48, 82, 83, 103
  transfer, 64, 79, 80, 81
  writing, 39, 41
Spence, ix, 52, 80, 105, 107
Standardized English, 9, 26, 32, 46, 49, 74
Stereotypes, 49
Synecdoche, 27, 28, 88

Tension, 28, 91
TESOL, 33, 103, 105, 106, 107
Thailand, 35, 36, 37, 38
Theme, 17, 18, 24, 28, 29, 30, 41, 50, 65, 87, 91, 100, 101
Transfer, 31, 41, 64, 79, 80, 81, 82, 84
Translation, 30, 41, 43
Topic, x, 5, 12, 13, 18, 28, 48, 51, 58, 72, 77, 80, 82, 91, 92, 93, 100

Valdés, 32, 106
VanSledright, 58, 106

Vivid language, 42, 66
Vocabulary
  academic, 22, 29, 33, 38, 75
  English, 8, 15, 33, 39, 40, 41
  School, 25
  Science, 57
  Teaching, 31, 40, 41, 44, 85, 91, 103
  Voice
    In Literature, 50, 51
    Of others, ix, 5, 6, 7, 13, 15, 16, 17, 19, 22, 23, 24, 25, 26, 33, 40, 43, 44, 48, 56, 57, 63, 64, 65, 66, 67, 68, 69, 94, 96, 97, 98, 102, 105
  Writing Trait, 3, 17, 68, 100
Voloshinov, ix, 106

Vygotsky, 22, 106
Word
  choice, 3, 30
  detectives, 84
  walls, 75, 84
World English, 46, 47, 48, 104
Writing
  conference, 7, 30, 31, 49, 51, 52, 53, 82, 85, 91, 92, 93, 94
  workshop, 7, 21, 72, 74, 75, 82, 92, 93, 105

Yore, 57, 106

Zone of proximal development, 22

www.ingramcontent.com/pod-product-compliance
Lightning Source LLC
Chambersburg PA
CBHW070629300426
44113CB00010B/1718